STUDY GUIDE

James J. Teevan
University of Western Ontario

Francine Rubin

INTRODUCTION TO SOCIOLOGY
A Canadian Focus

Sixth Edition

Edited by

James J. Teevan, *University of Western Ontario*
W.E. Hewitt, *University of Western Ontario*

Prentice Hall Allyn and Bacon Canada
Scarborough, Ontario

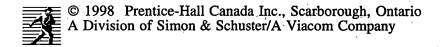
Acquisitions Editor: Rebecca Bersagel
Developmental Editor: Lisa Berland
Production Editor: Mary Ann McCutcheon
Production Coordinator: Jane Schell

1 2 3 4 5   W.   02 01 00 99 98

Printed and bound in Canada

Visit the Prentice Hall Canada Web site! Send us your comments, browse our catalogues, and more.
www.phcanada.com Or reach us through e-mail at **phabnfo_pubcanada@prenhall.com**

Contents

Preface

This *Study Guide* is designed for use with the sixth edition of *Introduction to Sociology: A Canadian Focus*, James J. Teevan and W.E. (Ted) Hewitt, editors. It provides students with study aids that complement the text.

For each chapter the following are included:

1.   *Chapter objectives:* a brief overview.

2.   *PH/CBC Video Clips* (where applicable): descriptions and discussion questions.

2.   *Key terms and definitions:* of the concepts introduced.

3.   *Self quiz:* multiple choice questions.

4.   *Fill in the blanks:* a further set of questions to facilitate learning.

5.   *Answers:* to the above.

CHAPTER 1

What Is Sociology?

OBJECTIVES

1.   To define sociology.

2.   To be able to distinguish sociology from the other social sciences.

3.   To be familiar with the historical background which led to the development of the discipline.

4.   To understand the major theoretical positions taken by sociologists to explain human interaction, including functionalist, conflict, symbolic interactionist, and feminist perspectives.

5.   To be familiar with the historical development of Canadian sociology.

KEY TERMS AND DEFINITIONS

1. _____: social sources or causes of behaviour used by sociologists to explain rates of behaviour in groups as opposed to individual behaviour.

2. _____: according to Durkheim, the suicide caused by feelings of being without limits, or boundlessness, a result of the relative lack of regulation found in some groups.

3. _____: the sociological model which portrays society as harmonious and as based on consensus.

4. _____: according to Durkheim, the suicide caused by the excessively strong integration found in some groups.

5. _____: Mead's term for individuals' attempts to put themselves in others' places and to imagine what these others are thinking, so as to make interaction with them easier.

6. _____: the sociological model that argues that individuals subjectively define and interpret their environments, that they are not fully constrained, and that they act from reasons rather than causes.

7. _____: according to Durkheim, the suicide caused by weak interpersonal ties, a result of the lack of integration found in some groups.

8. _____: the understanding as opposed to the predicting of behaviour.

9. _____: the sociological model which portrays society as marked by competition and/or exploitation.

10._____: according to Durkheim, the suicide caused by a decrease in options and feelings of being trapped, a result of the overregulation found in some groups.

11._____: the occasional minor, temporary disruptions in social life, as defined by functionalists.

12._____: seen by functionalist as the normal state of society, one marked by interdependence of parts and by harmony and consensus.

SELF-QUIZ

1.   One of the major concerns of sociology is

    a)   to explain individual sources of behaviour
    b)   cultural transmission and cultural uniformity
    c)   to explain how membership in social groups affects individual behaviour
    d)   deviant behaviour
    e)   to study the production and consumption of resources

2.   Social facts are

    a)   individual internal sources of behaviour
    b)   factors pertaining to group structures or to the interrelationships between individuals in groups
    c)   factors which may exist outside individual consciousness
    d)   factors which help people learn the content of a culture
    e)   *b* and *c*

3.   The type of suicide that men, Protestants, older people, and single people are more likely to commit is

    a)   fatalistic suicide
    b)   egoistic suicide
    c)   altruistic suicide
    d)   anomic suicide
    e)   alienated suicide

4.   Feminist approaches include each of the following except:

    a)   an examination of gender as one variable among many
    b)   looking at the informal and hidden aspects of social life
    c)   an examination of gender roles
    d)   a more interdisciplinary approach
    e)   acceptance of a variety of sociological models

5.   Scientific explanations can be characterized by the following:

    a)   intuition and faith
    b)   empirical testing and explanations of unique events
    c)   causal statements and common sense
    d)   simplicity and predictive ability
    e)   all of the above

6. Fatalistic suicide is most likely to occur in societies in which

   a) there are insufficient rules and regulations
   b) the regulations concerning sexual behaviour are lax
   c) there is enormous variation and conflict with regard to the content of norms, values, and roles
   d) people feel trapped, with insufficient alternatives
   e) b and c

7. Which of the following statements is not part of the functionalist perspective?

   a) large and complex societies are similar in structure to the human body
   b) social change is gradual and for the improvement of society
   c) the existence of cultural universals helps societies remain in equilibrium
   d) social arrangements persist because they benefit society
   e) society is marked by peace and consensus

8. Feminist sociology is least likely to take ideas from

   a) symbolic interactionism
   b) conflict sociology
   c) functionalism
   d) anglophone sociology
   e) francophone sociology

9. Scientific explanations should be simple, parsimonious, and elegant. Parsimonious means

   a) admirable as with a work of art
   b) generalizing rather than unique
   c) it is a synonym for empirical
   d) explaining the most with the least
   e) more pure than applied

10. Symbolic interactionism focuses on

    a) a macro-level of analysis
    b) the place of art in society
    c) cultural integration
    d) the autonomy of individuals
    e) group constraints

11. Weber, more than Durkheim, believed that sociology should include

    a) linguistic relativism
    b) subjective states of the individual
    c) mechanical solidarity
    d) a and c
    e) b and c

12. *Verstehen* is most closely associated with

    a) functionalism
    b) structural functionalism
    c) conflict theory
    d) equilibrium
    e) symbolic interactionism

FILL IN THE BLANKS

1. Durkheim believed that to understand behaviour, one must not only look at individual factors but also at such things as integration or the amount of regulation in society, factors he called _____.

2. The first question of feminist sociology is always _____?

3. Sociology is the study of social behaviour and relationships. It examines the effects of society and _____ upon human behaviour. Therefore, sociologists generally talk about _____ rates and _____ differences.

4. One result of the French and Industrial Revolutions was that simple, small, rural societies which were based upon tradition, became more _____ and _____, conditions which fostered the growth of sociology.

5. Auguste Comte, who is considered by some the founder of sociology, saw sociology as a secular religion as well as a science, with sociologists as _____.

6. Symbolic interactionists are more interested in _____ behaviour than in _____ behaviour.

7. The functionalist perspective adapted three major ideas from biology; they are _____, _____, and _____.

8. In contrast to functionalist theory, conflict theory generally argues that _____, _____, and _____, or radical social change, are the major forces in society.

9. Symbolic interactionism argues that people act on the basis of their individual perceptions not according to any _____.

10. George Herbert Mead, a symbolic interactionist thinker, argued that social interaction is made possible by the ability of individuals to engage in _____.

11. Sociology in both English and French Canada can trace its origin to Park at the University of Chicago and the _____ approach, the study of communities.

12. S. D. Clark, along with _____, who studied the production of staples such as fur and cod, and McLuhan, who examined _____, were important in the development of sociology at _____.

13. From a functionalist perspective, the scarcity of Canadian sociology teachers in the 1960s can be seen as a _____, one correctable by the importing of American sociologists, thus returning the system to a state of _____ .

14. Francophone sociology compared to its Anglophone counterpart is today more applied and more _____ in its orientation and as a consequence less _____.

15. The greatest cooperation between French and English sociology probably occurred with respect to research undertaken for the Royal Commission on _____.

Answers

KEY TERMS AND DEFINITIONS

1. social facts
2. anomic suicide
3. functionalism
4. altruistic suicide
5. role taking
6. symbolic interactionism
7. egoistic suicide
8. *verstehen*
9. conflict
10. fatalistic suicide
11. dysfunction
12. equilibrium

SELF QUIZ

1. c
2. e
3. b
4. a
5. d
6. d
7. c
8. c
9. d
10. d
11. b
12. e

FILL IN THE BLANKS

1. social facts
2. and what about the women
3. group membership, group, group
4. urbanized, heterogeneous
5. priests

6. understanding, predicting
7. function, equilibrium, development
8. power, disharmony, revolution
9. "objective" social reality
10. role taking
11. human ecology
12. Innis, media and communication, University of Toronto
13. dysfunction, equilibrium
14. macro-sociological, quantitative
15. Bilingualism and Biculturalism

CHAPTER 2

Research Methods

OBJECTIVES

1. To understand why sociologists conduct research and to appreciate the distinction between qualitative and quantitative methods.

2. To understand the workings of two major approaches — survey research and participant observation — on the following: theory, complexity of model, measurement, sampling, and data analysis, and to be able to compare and to know the advantages and disadvantages of each.

3. To be aware of other specific research alternatives, like experiments and content analysis, as well as some general approaches to methods including Marxist and female-friendly science.

KEY TERMS AND DEFINITIONS

1. _____ : a statistical demonstration that changes in one variable coincide with changes in another variable; not to be confused with cause.

2. _____ : the actual procedures used to measure a theoretical concept, as in I.Q. scores being used to measure intelligence.

3. _____: the degree to which a measure actually measures what it claims to measure.

4. _____: a method that extracts themes from communications, including letters, books, and newspapers.

5. _____: records produced by contemporaries of an event.

6. _____: explanations that arise from the data and are thus based on reality rather than on deductive logic.

7. _____: Marx's concept that research should not be *pure*, conducted for knowledge's sake, but *applied*, undertaken to improve society.

8. _____: interpretations of primary sources made by others not immediately present at an event.

9. _____: the type of research that takes place at one point in time as opposed to _____ research which, because it takes place over a period of time, can detect change and better demonstrate cause.

10._____: the derivation of a specific statement from a set of more general statements.

11._____: a sample in which every member of the population is eligible for inclusion and individuals are selected by chance.

12._____: the appearance that two variables are in a causal relationship, when in fact each is an effect of a common third variable.

13._____: the making of connecting links between related statements for deriving hypotheses.

14._____: repeating a research project in an attempt to verify earlier findings.

15._____: an experiment conducted in a real-life situation as opposed to a laboratory.

16._____: the degree to which repeated measurements of the same variable, using the same or equivalent instruments, are equal.

17._____: variables included in a model of behaviour that are neither independent nor dependent variables. They are held constant to check on apparent relationships between independent and dependent variables.

18._____: the group of subjects in an experiment that is exposed to the independent variable, as opposed to the _____ group which is not exposed.

19._____: a set of interrelated statements or propositions about a particular subject matter.

20._____: the generalizability of research results beyond the artificial laboratory experimental situation to the real world.

21._____: a characteristic, such as income or religion, that takes on different values among different individuals or groups. Those that are causes are generally called _____ and effects, _____.

22._____: a research strategy wherein a researcher becomes a member of a group to study it and group members are aware that they are being observed.

23._____: a statement of a presumed relationship between two or more variables.

24._____: the construction of a generalization from a set of specific statements.

25._____: a series of random samples taken in units of decreasing size, e.g., census tracts, then streets, then houses, then residents.

26._____: the examination by a researcher of someone else's data.

27._____: the systematic study of several cultures undertaken to compare them.

28._____: the application of natural science research methods to social science.

SELF QUIZ

1. The research process should probably be described as

   a) funnel-like and circular
   b) linear
   c) triangular
   d) expanding
   e) logarithmic

2. Positivists would most likely use _____ in deriving their hypotheses.

   a) the construction of a generalization from a set of specific statements
   b) post-hoc explanations which arise from the data
   c) deductive logic
   d) connecting links between related statements
      e) first-person explanations of behaviour

3. Validity refers to

   a) those measures of a dependent variable taken before, not after, the introduction of an independent variable
   b) the degree to which repeated measurements of the same variable with the same instruments are equal
   c) a characteristic which takes on different values among different individuals
   d) consistency in longitudinal research
   e) none of the above

4. Which of the following statements is true?

   a) if a measure is not reliable, it cannot be valid
   b) if a measure is reliable, it is also valid
   c) generalizability is more important than validity
   d) b and c only
   e) a and c only

5. For most people, peeling onions is a _____ cause of crying.

   a) necessary
   b) sufficient
   c) necessary and sufficient
   d) contributory
   e) adjunct

6. If researchers want to generalize to the total population and do not have to worry about costs, which of the following would be the best type of sample to draw upon?

a) systematic
b) accidental
c) quota
d) random
e) quasi-experimental

7. When examining tables, percentages allow more accurate comparisons than raw numbers. The only rule to remember about percentages is that

a)   each category of the dependent variable must add up to 100%
b)   each category of the independent variable must add up to 100%
c)   each category of the dependent variable must have equal cell sizes
d)   each category of the independent variable must have equal cell sizes
e)   b and d

8. Which research method attempts to keep the model quite simple by using random assignment and involving only the relevant independent and dependent variables?

a)   participant observation
b)   survey research
c)   content analysis
d)   experimental design
e)   ethnomethodology

9. If the distribution of your scores is skewed, or if you have an extreme value, or if your categories are open ended and you need a measure of central tendency, you probably should calculate a(n)

a)   mode
b)   mean
c)   median
d)   a and c
e)   average

10. Many participant observers refuse to derive hypotheses from theories, but instead use

a)   deductive logic
b)   grounded theory
c)   inductive logic
d)   a and b only
e)   b and c only

11. The issues of validity and generalizability are related and are at the heart of the debate between survey researchers and participant observers. Survey researchers argue that participant observation is inferior because

a)   of its difficulty in making generalizations
b)   of its operationalism
c)   it does not directly observe behaviour but elicits only verbal reports of that behaviour
d)   of its correlational nature
e)   c and d only

12.   Female-friendly science would probably be most opposed to

    a)   accepting personal experience
    b)   positivism
    c)   participant observation
    d)   interdisciplinary approaches
    e)   a breaking down of hierarchy

13.   Which of the following is true of experimental designs?

    a)   cause can be demonstrated more easily than in survey research or participant observation
    b)   it is strong in both generalizability and validity
    c)   studies are easily replicable
    d)   a and b only
    e)   a and c only

14.   Which method is least likely to be replicated?

    a)   the experiment
    b)   participant observation
    c)   survey research
    d)   content analysis
    e)   random digit dialing

15.   Content analysis is a less frequently used research method of sociology and involves extracting themes from communications. Among its major strengths is the fact that

    a)   it is inexpensive
    b)   it is strong on validity
    c)   it does not allow researchers to intrude upon the data
    d)   causal relationships can be demonstrated easily
    e)   a and c only

FILL IN THE BLANKS

1.   A list of all possible individual units in a population is called a _____.

2.   In the statement "as integration varies, suicide rates vary," integration is the _____ variable, and suicide rates the _____ variable.

3.   Hypothesizing that, since religious students are less deviant they will also be less likely to seek abortions, is an example of _____ logic.

4.   A _____ approach, which sees history as a series of conflicts over existing material arrangements, is attractive to Marxists. It maintains that the seeds for transformation exist in every society, with the new society containing seeds for its own transformation.

5. Whether crime should be measured by arrest rates, conviction rates, or victim surveys raises the issue of _____.

6. To examine whether the colour of the packaging influences ice cream sales for men and women separately would make gender the _____ variable.

7. You do not need a phone book if you draw your sample using _____.

8. There are only two rules of sampling; first, a sample should be _____ of the population from which it is drawn and second, conclusions should not be _____ beyond the groups from which the sample is drawn.

9. As a general rule, when analyzing data tables you should avoid examining actual numbers. _____ allow more accurate comparisons to be made.

10. Covert participant observation has a serious problem concerning _____.

11. In the most simple social science experiment there are two groups of subjects, the experimental and the control group. In a study of the effectiveness of a new drug, the _____ group would get the placebo, or sugar pill.

12. A crucial difference between survey research and experiments is that the effects of all other variables not included in experimental models are supposed to be eliminated through the _____ of subjects to groups.

13. Perspective rather than theory, subjectivity, and a complex picture of a small number of cases mean we are probably describing _____.

14. Noting that Bill, John, Nick, and other boys are more aggressive than Mary, Liz, Joan, and other girls and then concluding that boys are more aggressive than girls is an example of _____ theory.

15. In their disputes with survey researchers, participant observers, while admitting to limited generalizability due to their small samples, lay claim to greater _____ because they observe _____.

16. Survey research usually deals in correlations, demonstrations that changes in one variable coincide with changes in another. But variables may "go together" without the relation between them being _____.

17. Comparing experiments, survey research, and participant observation, validity is potentially strongest in _____. For generalizability, _____ may be best and the other two methods weaker. Finally, concerning cause, _____ excel and survey research is weaker.

18. Empathy and understanding are more characteristic of qualitative or quantitative methods? _____.

19. Because of their interest in social change, Marxists are more likely than functionalists to pay attention to _____ in their analysis.

20. In the examination of the relationship between alcohol consumption and date rape among 19-year-old males, _____ is the independent variable.

Answers

KEY TERMS AND DEFINITIONS

1. correlation
2. operational definition
3. validity
4. content analysis
5. primary sources
6. grounded theory
7. praxis
8. secondary sources
9. cross-sectional, longitudinal
10. deductive logic
11. random sample
12. spurious interpretation
13. axiomatic logic
14. replication
15. field experiment
16. reliability
17. control variables
18. experimental, control
19. theory
20. external validity
21. variable, independent, dependent
22. participant observation
23. hypothesis
24. inductive logic
25. cluster sampling
26. secondary analysis
27. comparative analysis
28. positivism

SELF QUIZ

1. a
2. c
3. e
4. a
5. b
6. d
7. b
8. d
9. c
10. e
11. a
12. b
13. e
14. b
15. e

FILL IN THE BLANKS

1. sampling frame
2. independent, dependent
3. deductive
4. dialectical
5. validity
6. control

7. random-digit dialing
8. representative, generalized
9. Percentages
10. ethics
11. control
12. random assignment
13. participant observation
14. grounded
15. validity, actual behaviour
16. causal
17. participant observation, survey research, experiments
18. qualitative
19. history
20. alcohol consumption

CHAPTER 3

Culture

OBJECTIVES

1.   To define culture and to distinguish and understand its major sociological aspects.

2.   To be aware of the existence of cultural variation and of arguments concerning cultural differences between the United States and Canada.

3.   To appreciate cultural integration, the scarcity of cultural universals, and the errors of ethnocentrism, especially its Eurocentric and androcentric variants.

4.   To understand four major theoretical perspectives used to explain cultural variation: functionalism, conflict theory, cultural materialism, and feminism.

PH/CBC VIDEO CLIP

"Cross Culture"
Source: *Venture*
Running Time: 5:55 minutes

In this video, corporate researcher Fons Trompenaars conducts a seminar on how to manage business affairs in a cross-cultural environment. The video reveals that Canadians in the corporate world have had to learn that understanding cultural differences has a significant impact on both communication and on generating contracts and commerce with potential and actual business contacts. The video examines the difficulties and challenges in negotiating business interactions between various cultures. Important concepts reviewed in this chapter—such as norms, mores, folkways, ethnocentrism, cultural relativism—are introduced and expanded upon in this video in a dynamic and interesting way.

Discussion questions

1.   Define in your terms your own culture. How does your particular culture affect or influence the work you have participated in or the travelling that you have experienced?

2.   Comment on some of the instances of communication breakdown that you have experienced, based on cultural differences between you and those you were attempting to communicate with. What were the cultural differences that influenced the dynamics of communication?

3.   The various theoretical approaches introduced in this text reappear in this chapter. By applying the frameworks of three major paradigms of sociological thought, comment on the examples presented in the video regarding communication breakdown based on culture.

KEY TERMS AND DEFINITIONS

1. _____: the sum total of all cultural elements associated with a given social group.

2. _____: a specific set of norms and values that the members of a society use to regulate some broad area of social life.

3. _____: those norms that when violated provoke a relatively strong reaction on the part of other group members.

4. _____: a subset of individuals within a society who are characterized by certain cultural elements that set them apart from others in the society.

5. _____: a group of people who reside in the same geographical area, who communicate extensively among themselves, and who share a common culture.

6. _____: anything that 1) is shared in common by the members of some social group; 2) is passed on to new members; and 3) in some way affects their behaviour or perceptions of the world. Three of the most important are values, norms, and roles.

7. _____: relatively general beliefs that define right and wrong, or that indicate general preferences.

8. _____: applied to culture, the theoretical perspective that explains cultural elements by showing how they contribute to societal stability.

9. _____: elements of culture found in all known societies.

10. _____: seeing things from the perspective of one's own culture. It includes the belief that one's own culture is superior to others and the belief that what is true of one's culture is true of others.

11. _____: stories of the recent past, told orally, which although believed to be true, are actually false and reflect unconscious fears.

12. _____: relatively precise rules specifying the behaviours permitted and those that are prohibited for group members.

13. _____: all the physical objects manufactured or used by the members of a society or a subculture.

14. _____: those norms that when violated do not provoke a strong reaction on the part of other group members.

15. _____: a cluster of behavioural expectations associated with some particular social position with a group or society.

16._____: the interrelationship of elements in a given culture such that a change in one element can lead to changes, sometimes unexpected, in other elements.

17._____: those preferences and objects that are widely distributed across all social classes in a society.

18._____: a theoretical perspective in which cultural elements are explained by showing how they are pragmatic and rational adaptations to the material environment.

19._____: a situation in which the behavioural expectations of one role are inconsistent with those of another concurrent role.

SELF QUIZ

1.   The insert about the Nuer and the father role could be used to illustrate the issue of

    a)   folkways versus mores
    b)   cultural universals, here that fathers generally must be males
    c)   avunculate
    d)   urban legends
    e)   structuralism

2.   If people simultaneously try to be parents of young children and full-time workers, they may experience

    a)   status enhancement
    b)   role conflict
    c)   cultural integration
    d)   anomic suicidal tendencies
    e)   egoistic suicidal tendencies

3.   Ethnocentrism includes

    a)   binary opposition
    b)   the assumption that what is true of your culture is also true of other cultures
    c)   the tendency to see your own culture as being "better" than other cultures
    d)   structuralism but not functionalism
    e)   b and c

4.   The major distinction between folkways and mores is

    a)   in the nature of the reaction that a violation of the norm produces and not in the content of the rule
    b)   in the content of the rule and not in the nature of the reaction that a violation of the norm produces
    c)   in the nature of the reaction that a violation of the norm produces and in the content of the rule
    d)   in neither the reaction nor the content
    e)   this question cannot be answered without more information

5. Which of the following most likely involves a violation of a folkway?

   a) childless couples
   b) income tax evasion
   c) having three spouses at the same time
   d) fatalistic suicide
   e) egoistic suicide

6. According to a conflict interpretation, Mother Theresa can be criticized for

   a) being too good and scaring others
   b) not helping enough in her native Yugoslavia
   c) deflecting attention from the real issue of inequality
   d) a and b
   e) a and c

7. Which of the following is false?

   a) most laws are social norms
   b) most social norms are laws
   c) many norms that structure behaviour are implicit
   d) a and c
   e) b and c

8. Barbie reinforces stereotypical female traits except with respect to

   a) being a wife and mother
   b) being well dressed
   c) being heterosexual
   d) her occupation
   e) being a consumer

9. Which of the following groups living in Canada could not constitute a subculture?

   a) Jews
   b) Italians
   c) Iranians
   d) Inuit
   e) a through d are all subcultures

10. Investigators of culture have consistently found that

    a) cultures exhibit enormous variation with regard to the content of their values, norms, and roles
    b) the elements of culture in a given society are often interrelated
    c) only a few cultural elements are common to all known societies
    d) a and b
    e) a, b, and c

11. According to Lipset, which of the following factors did not contribute to Canada's greater emphasis (in comparison to the American emphasis) on group harmony?

    a) Canada's strong ties to the British monarchy
    b) the U.S. and Canada's similar frontier experiences
    c) the dominant religion in English Canada being Anglican
    d) all of the above
    e) none of the above

12.   Which of the following can be classified as an object of popular culture?

   a)   a television set
   b)   a collection of Mozart's work
   c)   a Kentucky Fried Chicken franchise
   d)   an antique automobile
   e)   a and c only

13.   Lipstick messages on mirrors welcoming men to the world of AIDS were used to illustrate

   a)   urban legends
   b)   popular culture
   c)   cultural materialism
   d)   American versus Canadian value differences
   e)   mores

14.   Which perspective would explain a norm by showing how it contributes to the survival of the society in which it is found?

   a)   cultural materialism
   b)   functionalism
   c)   conflict sociology
   d)   symbolic interactionism
   e)   feminism

15.   Berdache is most closely associated with

   a)   religious sacrificial rites
   b)   fishing
   c)   the Arapesh
   d)   androcentricism
   e)   being two-spirited

FILL IN THE BLANKS

1.   The elements of culture that sociologists consider to be most important are

   _____, _____, and _____.

2.   Bans on the eating of pork and beef were used to illustrate the discussion of

   _____.

3.   The belief that all societies should have a leader or chief and a discussion of prehistoric Venuses were used to illustrate _____.

4.   The discussion of the wet-nurse was used to show that the _____, as we understand it, is not universal.

5.   The use of the term "hunting and gathering societies" rather than "gathering and hunting societies" can be used to illustrate the variety of ethnocentrism called

   _____.

6. Margaret Mead (1935) discovered cultural variation in the area of sex roles. In the Mundugamor society both males and females were expected to be _____. Among the Arapesh both sexes were expected to be _____. Among the Tchambuli _____ was associated with females and _____ with males.

7. Most social anthropologists during the nineteenth century believed that societies pass through three stages labeled _____, _____, and _____. Such ideas are an example of _____.

8. The first wave of feminist scholarship sought to add women as a focus of study. The second wave seeks more to challenge prevailing _____.

9. The disintegration of the Yir Yoront culture is an extreme example of the importance of _____.

10. Malinowski's explanation of the Trobrianders' use of magic in their ocean fishing uses the _____ perspective.

ANSWERS

KEY TERMS AND DEFINITIONS

1. culture
2. institution
3. mores
4. subculture
5. society
6. cultural element
7. values
8. functionalism
9. cultural universals
10. ethnocentrism
11. urban legends
12. norms
13. material culture
14. folkways
15. role
16. cultural integration
17. popular culture
18. cultural materialism
19. role conflict

SELF QUIZ

1. b
2. b
3. e
4. a
5. a
6. c
7. b
8. a
9. e
10. e
11. b
12. a
13. a
14. b
15. e

FILL IN THE BLANKS

1. values, norms, roles
2. cultural materialism
3. Eurocentrism
4. mother role
5. androcentrism
6. aggressive, passive, aggression, passivity
7. savagery, barbarism, civilization, ethnocentrism
8. research methods and conceptual frameworks
9. cultural integration
10. functionalist

CHAPTER 4

Socialization

OBJECTIVES

1. To understand the functions of socialization.

2. To understand the content and the limits of the nature versus nurture debate.

3. To understand and define the two major components of socialization, language and learning, and to describe their functions.

4. To understand the debate between the linguistic empiricists and linguistic nativists and its relation to the acquisition of language, thought, and culture.

5. To describe the learning of a culture and its importance to human development.

6. To understand three major theoretical approaches to socialization — psychodynamic, cognitive, and symbolic interactionist — as well as briefly describe the contributions of the major theorists found within each theoretical framework.

7. To be aware of the various agents of socialization and to understand the problems and implications involved in that complex process.

KEY TERMS AND DEFINITIONS

1. _____: the complex set of processes by which infants become distinct and unique individuals as well as members of society.

2. _____: the view that language is a reflection of one's cultural experiences and that language is not a factor that affects one's thought patterns in any unalterable way.

3. _____: the stage of moral development in which children believe that ethical rules are absolute, coming from some higher external authority; sometimes called moral realism.

4. _____: Cooley's expression for people's perceptions of how others see them.

5. _____: Mead's term for individuals' attempts to put themselves in others' places and to imagine what the others are thinking so as to make interaction with these others easier.

6. _____: the positive consequences individuals observe happening to others (especially a model) and which they expect will follow their own similar actions.

7. _____: the learning of the attitudes, beliefs, and behaviours that will be required for new roles individuals expect to play in the future.

8. _____: the major components of Freud's model of personality. The _____ is that aspect of personality which is impulsive, selfish, and pleasure-seeking. The _____ includes the intellectual and cognitive processes that make individuals unique. Most of it is conscious and guided by the reality principle: ideas and actions are modified to fit the real world. The _____ consists largely of what is called "conscience."

9. _____: the view that children have an innate capability to learn a language and do so as a function of natural maturation.

10. _____: any intimate personal acquaintance or specific prestigious person whose attitudes and opinions count for a great deal. Individuals take these people into account when evaluating their own actions.

11. _____: the debate over the extent to which human behaviour is affected by biological and genetic factors as opposed to social or environmental ones. Currently both factors are seen as contributing to the development of personality and the shaping of behaviour.

12. _____: the replacing of old attitudes, beliefs, and behaviours with new ones.

13. _____: the stage of moral development in which children see rules as products of deliberation and agreement rather than as absolute; sometimes called moral autonomy.

14. _____: the view that language is learned by reinforcement from others who already speak that language.

15. _____: the perspective that one's language determines and limits how one thinks and perceives.

16. _____: the conception of what is expected, of normative behaviour; individuals' unified conception of how the world views them.

17. _____: the negative consequences individuals observe happening to others (especially a model) and which they expect will follow their own similar actions.

18. _____: Mead's conception of the self contains two aspects: the first is the impulsive, creative aspect; the second is the reflective aspect that evaluates actions of the former.

SELF QUIZ

1.   The process of socialization refers to

   a)   learning
   b)   the process of becoming "human" and a member of society
   c)   factors which define behaviour by internal processes
   d)   social arrangements
   e)   the acquisition of language

2.   Which is a function of language?

   a)   to transmit
   b)   to integrate
   c)   to identify
   d)   a and c
   e)   b and c

3.   If, when comparing monozygotic to dizygotic twins, researchers found that the monozygotic twins were more similar to each other in their behaviour than the dizygotic twins, this would lend support to the contention that

   a)   environmental factors outweigh genetic factors
   b)   both genetic and environmental factors are involved
   c)   genetic factors outweigh environmental factors
   d)   the monozygotic twins had the exact same socialization experiences
   e)   the dizygotic twins were raised apart

4.   One function of socialization includes

   a)   development of an individual's personality
   b)   imitation
   c)   cultural transmission
   d)   developing the "I"
   e)   a and c

5.   Those who argue that children learn certain sounds and fail to learn others because the former are rewarded and the latter not rewarded would fall into the category of

   a)   linguistic empiricists
   b)   Freudians
   c)   linguistic nativists
   d)   linguistic positivists
   e)   symbolic interactionists

6.   A number of social scientists have argued that I.Q. tests are an imperfect measure of intelligence because I.Q. scores

   a)   vary over time
   b)   are subject to class-linked biases
   c)   don't really measure intelligence, but only certain aspects of I.Q.
   d)   a and b
   e)   b and c

7.   Defining dating as a rehearsal for playing marital roles illustrates the concept of

   a)   resocialization

b) anticipatory socialization
c) fixation
d) modelling
e) vicarious punishment

8. Socialization can be divided into several components. Which of the following is (are) not (a) major component(s) of the socialization process?

a) language
b) learning
c) role conflict
d) fixation
e) c and d only

9. The phallic or last stage identified by Freud would most likely come at the _____ stage identified by Piaget.

a) moral realism
b) morality of cooperation
c) morality of constraints
d) cognitive
e) a and b

10. In reference to language acquisition, the existence of a critical period would support the argument that

a) language is determined by cultural learning
b) language is determined by genetic factors
c) language is a function of both genetic and cultural factors
d) children learn a new language more slowly than adults
e) language determines thought

11. Bobo dolls were used in experiments to study

a) role conflict
b) morality of constraints
c) the imitation of aggression
d) resocialization
e) self-efficacy

12. Many new activities are learned through

a) vicarious reinforcement
b) modelling
c) fixation
d) a and c
e) a and b

13. The psychodynamic perspective focuses on

a) interactions with others and on the perceptions individuals have of these interactions
b) the development of individuals as members of various groups
c) the development of various internal characteristics and processes
d) social learning processes
e) vicarious punishment and reinforcement

14. Of Freud's three major components of personality, the one most likely to make you ignore others and take care of yourself is the
    - a) id
    - b) reality principle
    - c) superego
    - d) maternal instinct
    - e) ego

15. In reference to Erikson's theory of development, in adolescence individuals develop
    - a) trust
    - b) autonomy
    - c) initiative
    - d) industry
    - e) a sense of identity

16. Which of the following is a criticism of Freud's work?
    - a) his major constructs cannot be tested empirically
    - b) his concepts are not universal
    - c) he concentrated too heavily on vicarious punishment
    - d) his theories do not really tell us much about personality development
    - e) a and b only

17. Which theory argues that individuals constantly have a view or sense of themselves that is defined and affected by the actions and reactions of other people toward them?
    - a) Erikson's "psychological" theory
    - b) Freud's personality development theory
    - c) symbolic interactionism
    - d) modelling theory
    - e) none of the above

18. Cooley argued that an individual's self-concept is the result of
    - a) socialization
    - b) fixation
    - c) social interaction
    - d) the morality of constraints
    - e) vicarious reinforcement

19. The development of the self takes place in three stages according to Mead. Which of the following is part of Mead's theory?
    - a) the play stage
    - b) the latency stage
    - c) the symbolic stage
    - d) the looking-glass self stage
    - e) the reality stage

20. Children seem worst off if they come from homes marked by
    - a) divorce
    - b) death of a parent
    - c) single parenthood, that is, a never-married parent

    d)   separation
    e)   a and d

FILL IN THE BLANKS

1.   We can see the significance of socialization by comparing normal children with those raised in non-human environments. These children are often labelled feral because they act like _____.

2.   If we take a functionalist view, we can argue that socialization fulfills three major functions. They are _____, _____, and _____.

3.   Erikson identified _____ stages of ego development, from developing trust in infancy to evaluating one's life in old age.

4.   Finding that adopted children are more similar to their biological parents (from whom they have been separated) than to their adoptive parents would provide evidence for _____ contributions to personality development.

5.   Social scientists have uncovered evidence which suggests that genetic factors do influence certain personality traits. The text said that _____ and _____ are so influenced.

6.   Very young children believe in a morality of _____.

7.   Most of the ego is _____, and its interactions with the world are guided by the _____ principle.

8.   Prisoners often have to replace old roles and thoughts with new ones in order to become "good prisoners." This is an example of _____.

9.   Socialization can be divided into two major components. The most important process is _____.

10.   The _____ (Thomas, 1923) refers to the thought processes people use to interpret their environments. They may then act on these interpretations.

11.   Language systems have several common characteristics. The most important is that language is _____, that is, there are specific sounds and/or actions which represent something else.

12.   Language serves three major overlapping functions. These are to _____, to _____, and to _____.

13. Behaviour is a central element of a triad. Expected consequences come after behaviour while _____ precedes it.

14. The social and intellectual development of day-care children older than two years usually is _____ that of children raised by their mothers.

15. Freud's theory of personality development falls under the _____ theoretical perspective which focuses on the development of various internal characteristics and processes.

16. The mature personality develops through several stages, according to Freud. They are as follows: first is the _____ stage; second the _____ stage; third the _____ stage; fourth the _____ stage; and last the _____ stage.

17. The age group which watches the most television is _____, while _____ watch the least.

18. Mead argued that the development of self takes place in three stages. The first is the _____ stage in which infants simply imitate behaviour without understanding what they are doing. The second is the _____ stage in which children perform actual roles, and the third is the _____ stage in which a more unified conception of self emerges.

19. If at the end of what you consider a boring lecture you refrain from telling your teacher this view, the _____ aspect of the self is controlling your behaviour (Mead's term).

20. On Valentine's day you might send a card to your _____ other.

Answers

KEY TERMS AND DEFINITIONS

1. socialization
2. linguistic universalism
3. morality of constraints
4. looking-glass self
5. role taking
6. vicarious reinforcement
7. anticipatory socialization
8. id, ego, superego
9. linguistic nativism

10. significant other
11. nature versus nurture
12. resocialization
13. morality of cooperation
14. linguistic empiricism
15. linguistic relativism
16. generalized other
17. vicarious punishment
18. "I," "me"

SELF QUIZ

1.	b	8.	e	15.	e
2.	e	9.	b	16.	e
3.	c	10.	b	17.	c
4.	e	11.	c	18.	c
5.	a	12.	e	19.	a
6.	d	13.	c	20.	c
7.	b	14.	a		

FILL IN THE BLANKS

1. animals
2. the development of an individual's personality, cultural transmission, social integration
3. eight
4. genetic
5. extroversion and neuroticism
6. constraints
7. conscious, reality principle
8. resocialization
9. language
10. definition of the situation
11. symbolic
12. identify, integrate, socialize
13. context
14. similar to
15. psychodynamic
16. oral, anal, phallic, latency, genital
17. people over age 60, adolescents
18. preparatory, play, game
19. me
20. significant

CHAPTER 5

Deviance

OBJECTIVES

1. To understand what is meant by deviance and how societies decide what is deviant and what is not. The latter will include functionalist, conflict, and other explanations.

2. To understand how deviance is counted and the need for an audience reaction for deviance to exist.

3. To be familiar with social structural explanations of deviance and their limitations.

4. To be aware of the strengths and weaknesses of social process theories of deviance.

PH/CBC VIDEO CLIP

"School Violence"
Source: *Prime Time News*
Running Time: 11:25

Who are the most likely victims of crime today? A recent study revealed that people under the age of twenty four are three times more likely to be the victims of crime, much of which is violent crime that takes place in Canadian schools. This video addresses school violence by examining some of the problems inherent within high schools that contribute to making these offenses possible and by offering some solutions. A realistic reenactment of a violent incident that occurred at a high school in Langdon, British Columbia, is shown. A panel comprised of a Grade 11 student from Agincourt High School in Toronto, a member of the Canadian Association for Safe Schools, a defence lawyer, and a detective from the Metro Toronto Street Crime Unit discuss why so many Canadian schools today are unsafe and the consequences of that condition.

Discussion questions

1. Many teenagers are seeking peer acceptance and a sense of belonging through membership in violent gangs. Comment on this trend in light of the video reenactment.

2. Detective John Hughes of the Metro Toronto Street Crime Unit points out during the panel discussion in the video that there have been drastic changes in the types of violence that are occurring in greater frequency in urban centres. What are some of these changes mentioned?

3. Comment on how the structural-functional paradigm, the symbolic-interaction paradigm, and social-conflict theory can be applied to this particular reenactment.

4.   If you have experienced an incident of school violence, comment on it from a personal point of view and a theoretical perspective.

5.   What are some of the advantages and disadvantages of a "zero tolerance" mandate, as expressed by the individuals on the panel?

KEY TERMS AND DEFINITIONS

1. _____: the explanation that views the widespread discrepancy between a society's goals and the legitimate means it provides to achieve those goals as leading to normlessness and eventually to deviance.

2. _____: the view that the economic elite is the single major force behind definitions of what is and what is not deviant.

3. _____: body types (thin, fat, and muscular respectively) tested for their relationship to personality and then to crime and delinquency.

4. _____: the explanation of deviance which argues that societal reactions to minor deviance may alienate those so stigmatized and may cut off their options for conformity, thus leading to greater deviance as an adaptation to the stigma.

5. _____: Merton's four deviant adaptations to the problems created when society provides insufficient means to achieve its goals are: _____ who find illegitimate means, _____ who water down goals, _____ who give up goals and means, and _____ who seek both new goals and new means.

6. _____: a process whereby an individual's deviance becomes a master status. Good traits are ignored or misinterpreted, while bad ones are magnified out of proportion.

7. _____: a theory that sees deviance as learned in small-group interaction, wherein an individual internalizes an excess of pro-deviant perspectives.

8. _____: deviant acts committed prior to any social reaction. They arise from a variety of sources.

9. _____: the deviance which arises out of anger, alienation, limiting of options, and change of self concept that may occur after a negative social reaction or labelling.

10. _____: applied by society to those actors it considers deviant, it is the redefinition of their past behaviours as deviant as well.

11._____: those who commit deviant acts but to whom no one responds as if they have done so, either because they are not caught, or if caught, because they are excused for some reason.

12._____: Durkheim's term for the set of agreed upon standards of society assumed to have arisen from consensus.

13._____: people who seek to influence the making of rules and definitions of deviance.

14._____: an argument stating that punishing individuals for minor forms of deviance may backfire and encourage them to take up deviant careers.

15._____: the view that power is shared and that definitions of deviance arise not from consensus, nor from any one group, but from a diversity of sources.

16._____: a way of life in opposition to, as opposed to merely distinct from, the larger culture.

17._____: calling attention to minor acts of deviance which could encourage more major forms of deviance.

18._____: rationalizations that allow deviants to define their behaviour as acceptable.

19._____: conditions or behaviour perceived by society as not normal and at least somewhat disvalued and thus an acceptable target for social control.

SELF QUIZ

1. In arguing that stores can afford a bit of shoplifting, a thief is using which technique of neutralization?

   a) denial of personal responsibility
   b) denial of injury
   c) condemning the condemners
   d) denial of the victim
   e) appeal to higher loyalties

2. Commitment, beliefs, involvement, and attachment should remind you of _____ theory.

   a) social control
   b) anomie
   c) labelling
   d) psychological
   e) critical

3. According to functionalists, definitions of deviance come from

   a) moral entrepreneurs
   b) the collective conscience
   c) false consciousness
   d) the proletariat (working class)
   e) the economic elite

4. Which of the following groups do not exceed their opposites in mental illness rates?

   a) the young
   b) males
   c) urban areas
   d) the poor
   e) the divorced

5. Sheldon sought explanations for crime in biology and hypothesized that biological variables, especially body type, lead to personality variables which in turn lead to crime. He argued that _____ are more likely to commit crimes.

   a) ectomorphs
   b) mesomorphs
   c) endomorphs
   d) individuals with XYY chromosomes
   e) none of the above, all body types are equal in their criminality

6. Biological explanations of deviance are criticized for

   a) often ignoring women
   b) being atavistic
   c) being unable to account for fluctuations over time of deviance rates
   d) b and c
   e) a and c

7. Arguing that you learned to shoplift because your friends taught you that such behaviour is acceptable would be consistent with _____ theory.

   a) anomie
   b) differential association
   c) labelling
   d) deviance amplification
   e) relative deprivation

8. According to Smith, which of the following (is) are not (a) correlate(s) of the physical forms of wife abuse?

   a) unemployment of husband
   b) low family income
   c) low educational achievement of husband
   d) low educational achievement of wife
   e) ethnicity and religious affiliation

9.   Although Merton's theory of anomie is flawed, its greatest contribution to the study of deviance is its argument

    a)   that social factors are important in explaining individual deviance
    b)   that deviance is caused by biological, psychological, *and* social factors
    c)   that deviance does not exist without a reaction
    d)   that calling attention to minor acts of deviance may encourage major forms of deviance
    e)   none of the above

10.   Which of the following is not a major point of the labelling perspective?

    a)   individuals are neither totally deviant nor totally conformist but instead possess aspects of both
    b)   labelling and punishing individuals may lead to more and not less deviance
    c)   deviance is learned, usually alone, but sometimes with others
    d)   an individual may become the victim of role engulfment
    e)   part of the anger among those labeled concerns the existence of rule-breakers

11.   Looking at the crimes of the powerful would most likely be the concern of a(n) _____ theorist.

    a)   anomie
    b)   differential association
    c)   functionalist
    d)   radical
    e)   psychological

12.   Arguments against collecting crime statistics by race and ethnic categories did not include

    a)   difficulties in measuring race and ethnicity
    b)   the need to examine social class factors
    c)   the fact that some types of crimes do not get full police attention
    d)   the fact that deviance needs a reaction as well as an action
    e)   a and b

13.   Labelling theorists can be placed into the larger theoretical perspective of _____ since they argue that the deviant's definitions of self and of the situation are crucial.

    a)   social structure
    b)   conflict theory
    c)   symbolic interactionism
    d)   functionalism
    e)   pluralism

14.   Which of the following individuals is more likely to commit a crime?

    a)   a young female in Prince Edward Island who comes from a disadvantaged background
    b)   an older male in an urban area in British Columbia
    c)   a young male in New Brunswick with a grade 12 education
    d)   a young female in a rural area with a grade 8 education
    e)   a young male in Alberta with a grade 6 education

15. According to functionalism, deviance can benefit society in which of the following ways?

    a) deviance may begin a process of adaptation and progress to new and better norms and values

    b) deviance may aid in the process of greater social equality

    c) deviance helps unify the different layers of society since almost everyone commits a deviant act at one time or another

    d) a and c only

    e) b and c only

FILL IN THE BLANKS

1. The different definitions of deviance found among the Inuit society compared with the rest of Canada illustrate the relative definition of deviance, that what is deviant is specific to _____, _____, and _____.

2. Halloween, smoke detectors, and the bottom layer of society were each mentioned in the discussion of _____.

3. A problem with anomie and social control theories is that in the former, one would expect _____ to have high crime rates because they often are denied means, but they do not, and in the latter, the _____ to have high crime rates because they are often alone, but they do not.

4. The highest crime rates provincially are found in _____, _____, and _____.

5. Freudians might see mental illness as due to the inability of the _____ to handle conflicts among the id, the superego and the external world.

6. Widespread fluctuations this century in crime, alcoholism, and mental illness rates cast doubt on _____ explanations of deviance.

7. Merton argued that the discrepancy between the goals a society instills and the acceptable means the society provides to achieve the goals can lead to a state of _____, a large-scale breakdown of rules which he called _____.

8. Working class people who live in modest homes, have older cars, and take few vacations are called _____ according to Merton's scheme.

9. The _____ approach which focused on cities and urban social disorganization preceded more formal sociological attempts to explain crime.

10. Hagan, Gillis, and Chan examined police and self-report juvenile delinquency data for an Ontario city and concluded that there is evidence of some _____, that the police expect more delinquency in _____ areas, look for it there, and then find that greater amount in a self-fulfilling prophecy.

11. In general the _____ may be more frequently labelled for minor acts of crime and delinquency than the _____, but for serious forms this bias may be less important.

12. Some criminologists accept the argument of _____, that those who suffer crime may play a part in the process, making them the specific targets of criminals.

13. Cohen's delinquent boys, according to the text, are closest to Merton's _____.

14. The need for a reaction as well as an action for deviance led to a discussion of _____ versus _____, the former being those not caught for their deviance, the latter being those caught.

15. A focus on the coming together in time and space of victims, criminals, and a lack of social control is the main point of the _____ explanation of crime.

ANSWERS

KEY TERMS AND DEFINITIONS

1. anomie
2. critical school
3. ectomorphs, endomorphs, mesomorphs
4. labelling theory
5. innovators, ritualists, retreatists, rebels
6. role engulfment
7. differential association
8. primary deviance
9. secondary deviance
10. retrospective interpretation
11. rule-breakers
12. collective conscience
13. moral entrepreneurs
14. deviance amplifying process
15. pluralism
16. contraculture
17. dramatization of evil
18. techniques of neutralization
19. deviance

SELF QUIZ

1. b
2. a
3. b
4. a
5. b

6. e
7. b
8. e
9. a
10. c

11. d
12. b
13. c
14. e
15. a

FILL IN THE BLANKS

1. time, place, circumstance
2. the functions of deviance
3. women, the elderly
4. Territories, BC, and Alberta
5. ego
6. biological
7. normlessness, anomie
8. ritualists
9. human ecology
10. bias, poorer
11. powerless, powerful
12. victim precipitation
13. rebels
14. rule breakers, deviants
15. routine activities approach

CHAPTER 6

Gender Relations

OBJECTIVES

1.   To understand gender from a social, macro-perspective called the gendered order, and from an individual perspective called gendered identity.

2.   To appreciate the major theoretical perspectives now being applied to the study of gender.

3.   To extend to gender roles the discussion of the nature-nurture debate developed in the socialization chapter.

4.   To be familiar with the processes involved in gender socialization, including the role of language.

5.   To be aware of the relationship between gender and such variables as work, health, aging, deviance, and poverty.

PH/CBC VIDEO CLIP

"Same Sex, Same Rights?"
Source: *Prime Time News*
Running Time: 6:20 minutes

Are same-sex rights, entitlements, and benefits simply part of the legislation offering equality to homosexuals or are these demands part of a movement that strikes at the foundation of the so-called traditional family? This video gives an historical and contemporary account of discrimination against homosexuals in Canada. As well, the video offers film footage of the first gay demonstrations and gay pride weeks in Canada. Legal ramifications of discrimination based on sexual orientation are discussed by Barbara Finley, a Vancouver gay rights lawyer.

Discussion questions

1.   As Barbara Finley argues, there is no jurisdiction in Canada with statutes in which sexual orientation protection includes partnerships. But the courts have been finding that sexual orientation protection does include partnerships. What are your thoughts on this contentious issue?

2.   Do you think that Bill 167 is really more a battle over legitimacy for gays and lesbians in Canada, rather than active legislature for same-sex benefits?

3.   How might some of the issues presented in Chapter 6 be applied to the existence of heterosexism?

4. Comment on the volatile issue of same-sex rights, benefits, and entitlements, grounding your response in functionalist, conflict, symbolic interactionist, and/or feminist theoretical frameworks.

KEY TERMS AND DEFINITIONS

1. _____: the system of male dominance, through which males are systematically accorded greater access to resources and women are systematically oppressed.

2. _____: the tendency to communicate sexist messages, such as male superiority or the assumption that certain roles must be occupied by either males or females, through one's use of language.

3. _____: the process of acquiring a gendered identity.

4. _____: role differentiation in which males and females are segregated, according to their sex, in the spheres of both paid and unpaid labour according to the belief that certain tasks are more appropriate for one sex than the other.

5. _____: the view that women's real strength lies in their reproductive capacities, and that women's roles as wives and mothers are their true calling and source of status.

6. _____: the set of traits including emotionality, passivity, and weakness, seen by functionalists as associated with female roles of unpaid wife, mother, and homemaker, particularly as limited to the private sphere.

7. _____: the dual segregation of women into the pink-collar occupations outside the home, and to unpaid labour inside the home.

8. _____: the view that equality between the sexes can be achieved only through the abolition of male supremacy. Some of its advocates argue for female separatism, and the abdication of women's reproductive role as the route to liberation.

9. _____: a biological category, either male or female, referring to physiological differences, the most pronounced of which involve the reproductive organs and body size.

10. _____: the view that gender inequality has its roots in the combined oppressiveness of patriarchy and capitalism.

11. _____: the tendency in Canadian society for women at all stages of the adult life cycle to be poorer than men, and to be trapped in lives of poverty.

12._____: as used by sociologists and others, a social category, either masculine or feminine, referring to the social expectations developed and placed upon individuals on the basis of their biological sex.

13._____: the self as it develops in accordance with the individual's gender and the social definitions of that gender within the larger gendered order.

14._____: the widely held belief that females and males in our society are exclusively heterosexual, leading to labels of deviance if it is discovered they are not.

15._____: the widespread belief and understanding that males are superior to females: that they are more entitled to make decisions, to control resources, and generally to be in positions of authority.

16._____: the set of norms specifying appropriate behaviour for males and females; those who violate them are generally labelled deviant.

17._____: the sphere of unpaid domestic labour and biological reproduction, seen from a functionalist perspective as the preserve of females.

18._____: the set of structural relations through which individual members of society are accorded differential treatment on the basis of their gender.

19._____: the set of traits including rationality, aggression, and strength, seen by functionalists to be associated with the male roles of breadwinner and disciplinarian, particularly as limited to the public sphere.

20._____: the view that most structural inequality between women and men can be eradicated through the making of laws and the creation of social policies which will alter power relationships.

21._____: the sphere of paid labour and commerce, seen from a functionalist perspective as the preserve of males.

SELF QUIZ

1.   The terms masculine and feminine are most closely associated with the concept of

   a)   sex
   b)   gendered order rather than gendered identity
   c)   gender
   d)   ascribed status
   e)   transsexuality

2.   The position most likely to define a gendered division of labour as acceptable is

   a)   symbolic interactionism
   b)   feminism

    c) socialist feminism
    d) radical feminism
    e) functionalism

3. Instrumentality does not include

    a) rationality
    b) aggression
    c) strength and domination
    d) emotionality
    e) breadwinning

4. Concerning sex-change operations, which of the following is false?

    a) there are more male to female, than female to male operations
    b) electrolysis and estrogen may be used
    c) among men undergoing the operation, the greatest proportion are homosexuals
        and transvestites
    d) some men seek the operation to avoid the stigma of homosexuality
    e) an artificial penis may be constructed

5. Marx tended to a take a position similar to _____ on the question of the
    gendered division of labour.

    a) functionalists
    b) symbolic interactionists
    c) radical feminists
    d) liberal feminists
    e) the nurture side

6. A focus on day care and pay equity would be most characteristic of _____
    feminism.

    a) maternal
    b) liberal
    c) socialist
    d) radical
    e) a to d are all the same on these issues

7. Which was not listed as a myth of male/female differences?

    a) boys are innately more independent than girls
    b) girls have better verbal ability
    c) boys are more aggressive
    d) women experience more eating disorders than men do
    e) male and female brains are organized differently

8. Which term is out of place with the others?

    a) heterosexual assumption
    b) gendered division of labour
    c) pink ghetto
    d) gender inclusive language
    e) feminization of poverty

9. Homeless women are drawn heavily from among
    a) former mental patients
    b) teenage runaways
    c) wives of homeless men
    d) a and b
    e) b and c

10. Women are in the majority for all of the following employee categories except
    a) sales
    b) clerical
    c) nurses
    d) service
    e) teaching

11. Even in 1991, women made only about _____ of what men did.
    a) 50%
    b) 30%
    c) 90%
    d) 50%
    e) 70%

12. In health matters women do better than men in all of the following except
    a) declining smoking rates
    b) amount of stress experienced
    c) ability to handle stress
    d) exposure to poor work conditions
    e) longevity

13. Of the following the most general term is
    a) gender norms
    b) ideology of gender inequality
    c) gendered order
    d) gender inclusive language
    e) double ghetto

14. Penis, vagina, testes mean that we are talking about
    a) gender
    b) sex
    c) masculine and feminine
    d) gender identity
    e) homosexuality

15. Identification as a transsexual would probably be best explained using
    a) maternal feminism
    b) conflict theory
    c) functionalism
    d) symbolic interactionism
    e) a and b

FILL IN THE BLANKS

1.   The _____ is socially reproduced through the process of gender socialization.

2.   It can be argued that sex is an _____ characteristic while gender is an _____ characteristic.

3.   A major criticism of the functionalist view is that it justifies _____.

4.   Going to work is an _____ task while nurturing is an _____ task.

5.   A patriarch plus a homemaker and children would describe the Parsonian _____ family.

6.   Transsexuals have a discrepancy between their gender identity and their biological sex. This is much more than _____, or wearing clothes of the other sex.

7.   Unlike functionalism, symbolic interactionism focuses on the _____ of the different roles allocated to males and females.

8.   _____ feminism is associated with a search for alternative reproductive strategies.

9.   Women's work can be divided into three categories, _____, _____, and _____.

10.   The term for Devor's masculine-appearing women is _____.

11.   It is estimated that in China _____ females are "missing."

12.   Bulimia and anorexia nervosa are manifestations of the _____ in which women's self worth is particularly defined through their appearance.

13.   On the good side, the "discovery" of _____ has led to the setting up of clinics to reduce its effects. On the bad side it can be used to legitimate unequal treatment of men and women.

14.   Approximately _____ percent of one-parent households are headed by females.

15.   Of the four types of feminism listed, a religious conservative would most likely adopt _____.

Answers

KEY TERMS AND DEFINITIONS

1.   patriarchy
2.   linguistic sexism
3.   gender socialization
4.   gendered division of labour
5.   maternal feminism
6.   expressive dimension
7.   double ghetto
8.   radical feminism
9.   sex
10.   socialist feminism
11.   feminization of poverty

12.   gender
13.   gendered identity
14.   heterosexual assumption
15.   ideology of gender inequality
16.   gender norms
17.   private realm
18.   gendered order
19.   instrumental dimension
20.   liberal feminism
21.   public realm

SELF QUIZ

1.   c
2.   e
3.   d
4.   c
5.   a

6.   b
7.   d
8.   d
9.   d
10.   a

11.   e
12.   a
13.   c
14.   b
15.   d

FILL IN THE BLANKS

1.   gendered order
2.   ascribed, achieved
3.   an ideology of gender inequality
4.   instrumental, expressive
5.   head-complement
6.   transvestism
7.   social construction
8.   Radical
9.   wifework, motherwork, housework
10.   gender blenders

11.   30 million
12.   cult of thinness
13.   PMS
14.   80 (82)
15.   maternal feminism

CHAPTER 7

Social Stratification

OBJECTIVES

1. To understand the basic concepts and definitions involved in the study of social stratification: status, stratum, status hierarchies and power dimensions, ascribed and achieved status, social mobility, class, and social class.

2. To understand several of the major theories of social stratification including Marxist, Weberian, and structural-functionalist positions.

3. To be aware of Canada's stratification structure, including the eight most important factors of social differentiation and their interrelationships: wealth and property, occupation, education, race/ethnicity, region and rural-urban location, gender, age, and political power.

4. To be aware of some of the major consequences of stratification for people, including its effects on life chances, life-styles, values, and beliefs.

PH/CBC VIDEO CLIPS

"Portraits From a Project"
Source: *Prime Time News*
Running Time: 4:30 minutes

How do the over one million Canadian families who live in poverty exist? How do they find the means to cope with their struggles, both financially and emotionally? *Portraits from a Project* explores life in Heatherington, a subsidized housing project in Ottawa, Ontario, which almost three hundred poor families call home. This video clip will introduce you to some of the people who live in Heatherington by highlighting their day-to-day lives. As well, we will view short excerpts of a play that some of the parents of Heatherington have produced and staged for government agencies, to demonstrate to outsiders what life inside Heatherington is actually like. In this heart-rending video, we will hear about a provincial government program called "Better Beginnings–Better Futures" which offers help and hope. The concept behind "Better Beginnings" is, in a community setting, to reduce long-term emotional and behavioural problems and promote optimal development in children and adolescents.

Discussion questions

1. No single description encompasses the lives of all poor people. Age, education, race and ethnicity, gender, and family patterns are all factors that contribute to the divergent profile of poverty. Discuss some of the psychological and social stigmatization that are experienced by some adults and children who live in poverty.

2.   What are some of the social, psychological, and physical outlets demonstrated in the video that assist the children of subsidized housing communities such as Heatherington?

3.   Comment on the social and psychological benefits of the Ontario government program "Better Beginnings–Better Futures," which is aimed at helping the children who live in subsidized housing communities such as Heatherington.

4.   How does a program such as "Better Beginnings–Better Futures" involve a community such as Heatherington in raising healthy children?

KEY TERMS AND DEFINITIONS

1. _____: a set of individuals sharing a similar economic status or market position.

2. _____: Marx's word for the working class, the non-owners of the means of production.

3. _____: the combination of statuses that any one individual occupies.

4. _____: Weber's three (as opposed to Marx's one) bases of _____ social inequality.

5. _____: movement or change between parental status and a child's status in the same status hierarchy.

6. _____: movement up and down a status hierarchy.

7. _____: a position in a status hierarchy which is attained by individual effort or accomplishment.

8. _____: a Marxian category including people who share the same economic position but who may be unaware of their common class position.

9. _____: the tendency for diversification and complexity in the statuses and characteristics of social life.

10. _____: any one of a set of rankings along which statuses are rated in terms of their power.

11. _____: movement by an individual from one status to another of similar rank within the same status hierarchy.

12. _____: any position occupied by an individual in a social system.

13. _____: a set of statuses of similar rank in any status hierarchy.

14._____: the capitalist class, as defined by Marx. The _____ were the small-property owners, a group he predicted would be swallowed by the larger capitalists.

15._____: sometimes called domination, it becomes a regular part of everyday human existence, usually because it is established in formal laws or accepted customs.

16._____: dissimilarity in the rankings of an individual's statuses in a set of status hierarchies.

17._____: a position in a status hierarchy that is inherited or assigned.

18._____: movement by an individual from one status to another in the same status hierarchy during a lifetime or career.

19._____: similarity in the rankings of an individual's statuses in a set of status hierarchies.

20._____: a Marxian category including people who share the same economic position, are aware of their common class position, and who thus may become agents for social change.

21._____: a category of individuals who possess similar economic position as well as group consciousness, common identity, and a tendency to act as a social unit.

22._____: the general pattern of inequality or ranking, of socially differentiated characteristics.

23._____: a differential capacity to command resources and thereby control social situations.

SELF QUIZ

1.　It as been argued that the study of social stratification is concerned mainly with "who gets what and why." In this view social stratification is

　　a)　independent of power
　　b)　a distributive process
　　c)　an example of capitalism in its purest form
　　d)　concerned with class for itself not class in itself
　　e)　a study of the micro-elements in society

2.　Concerning status consistency, which is true?

　　a)　it probably relates more to wealth than to occupation
　　b)　status consistency is almost never found
　　c)　a high degree of status consistency tends to indicate a "closed" stratification system
　　d)　it relates mainly to ascribed statuses
　　e)　it relates mainly to achieved statuses

3.   Which of the following is (are) (an) ascribed status?

   a)   educational status
   b)   ethnic origin
   c)   occupational status
   d)   a and b
   e)   a, b, and c

4.   Power which arises largely from control over human resources or the activities of other people is _____ power.

   a)   economic
   b)   political
   c)   ideological
   d)   institutionalized
   e)   domination

5.   For Marx, apart from obvious differences in wealth and prestige, what really underlies the division of societies into two opposing groups is

   a)   the power that derives from ownership or non-ownership of property
   b)   the proletariat and the bourgeoisie
   c)   the structure and the superstructure
   d)   class for itself and class in itself
   e)   none of the above

6.   Marx did not advocate

   a)   equal liability of all to labour
   b)   centralization of credit
   c)   a graduated income tax
   d)   the continued distinction between town and country
   e)   free education

7.   Weber's concept of power in social organizational theory can best be labeled

   a)   conflict
   b)   functional
   c)   pluralist
   d)   symbolic interactionist
   e)   positivist

8.   Attaching greater rewards to those positions either deemed crucial or requiring rare skills than to less valuable ones is a part of which perspective?

   a)   structural-functionalism
   b)   symbolic interactionism
   c)   pluralism
   d)   conflict
   e)   none of the above

9.   In societies such as Canada, in which wealth and property can be inherited, there is a tendency toward reduced

   a)   horizontal mobility
   b)   status consistency
   c)   vertical social mobility

d) generational conflict
e) class structure

10. Which of the following is true concerning Canada's income distribution?

a) income is more widely diffused in the population today than ever before
b) the distribution of wealth has not changed very much in recent decades
c) government programs to redistribute income from the very rich to the lower strata have generally been successful
d) the upper strata received relatively less income in the 1990s than in the 1950s
e) c and d

11. The best single indicator of an individual's general stratum position is

a) income
b) education
c) ethnicity
d) sex
e) occupation

12. Which of the following statements is true?

a) there is an equal opportunity for all citizens in Canadian society to acquire education
b) in Canada today, ascriptive traits are still related to educational achievement, although perhaps less so than historically
c) inequality of access has little to do with the differences in education levels among the population
d) Canada's universal access to education has guaranteed an open stratification system
e) a and d only

13. According to Porter, Canada resembles a "vertical mosaic," a

a) social structure marked by a high degree of status consistency
b) social structure in which wealth and property can be passed on through inheritance
c) social structure in which the distribution of wealth is increasingly more widely diffused among various racial and ethnic groups
d) social structure comprising many diverse racial and ethnic groups, ranked along a hierarchy of power and privilege
e) social structure in which enormous variation exists in the ranking of various norms and values

14. During the so-called "Quiet Revolution," there was a concerted move in Quebec toward *rattrapage*, referring to

a) the religious values of French Canadians which put them at a disadvantage in the competition for material success
b) catching up with English Canada
c) a decline in ethnic prejudice and discrimination in Quebec
d) the beginning of the political movement of the *Parti Québécois*
e) an emphasis on bilingualism and biculturalism

15. Which of the following is not a characteristic of a metropolis as opposed to a hinterland?

    a) seat of political power
    b) large-scale industry
    c) large universities
    d) source of raw materials
    e) population centre

16. Which of the following is false?

    a) women made up over 45% of the labour force in 1991
    b) among full-time employees, women make only 72% of the average male wage
    c) women's lower pay is largely a function of their lesser training and experience
    d) the female disadvantage in pay is more evident among older cohorts
    e) a through d are false

17. It would appear that political power is associated with the other sources of power which determine the distribution of wealth, prestige, and other resources in this country. Those who tend to dominate are

    a) of foreign origin and live outside Canada
    b) male and of French origin
    c) the economic elites who live in hinterland areas
    d) central Canadians, of British origin, and male
    e) central Canadians and of French origin

18. Which of the following statements is true in reference to social stratification?

    a) because they have more to spend, people from the middle and upper strata are more likely to place a greater emphasis on home life than those from the lower strata
    b) lower-class individuals are more susceptible to a broad spectrum of physical and mental illnesses than their more prosperous counterparts
    c) the working class tends to place less value than its counterparts on material success and financial security
    d) daily life in the upper strata is characterized by greater restrictiveness than life in the lower strata
    e) a and b

FILL IN THE BLANKS

1. Various government programs to redistribute wealth to the lower strata usually do so at the expense of the _____.

2. Evidence indicates that the top 10 percent of the Canadian population holds over _____ of all wealth. Both stocks and dividends are disproportionately theirs.

3. According to Marx, history is a series of struggles between haves and have-nots, today capitalist and worker, previously _____ and _____, and before that _____ and _____.

4. Most researchers suggest that age has an up-and-down, or _____, association with stratification.

5. We usually discuss _____ mobility as most indicative of an open stratification system.

6. If, as a group, manual labourers were to have similar economic power, they would constitute a _____.

7. Probably the greatest wealth is found in the province of _____, while the least is found in the _____ provinces.

8. Marx focused on private ownership of productive property, or what he called the _____.

9. For socialism to triumph, the working class has to become more than just a _____, a category of people sharing the same economic position. In addition, it needs an awareness of its common position and a willingness to mobilize for change if it is to become a genuine _____.

10. Marx suggested that two stages follow the revolution of the proletariat: first, a _____ phase, a dictatorship of the proletariat with the leaders of the revolution heading the political apparatus or the state. In the second stage, _____ is achieved and the state as a political force withers away.

11. While Marx stressed conflict, group (class) action, and the singular importance of economic power in understanding social stratification, the structural-functionalist school of thought emphasizes instead _____, _____, and _____ of power in modern social structures.

12. The author of the chapter, in agreement with Marx, argues that control of property and wealth, particularly by large businesses, is the most important source of _____ in modern stratification systems. In addition, following Weber, he suggests that the other two socioeconomic status hierarchies, _____ and _____, also play a key role in shaping the system of inequality.

13. The distribution of _____ is the most direct measure or indication of how groups or individuals rank in the overall stratification system.

14. The biggest occupational change this century has been the growth of _____ occupations and the corresponding decline of people working in _____.

15. In 1990, university graduates made about _____ as much in total income as did high school graduates.

16. The major subsystems, or _____ of society include the economy, polity, religion, education, and agents of social control.

17. Education is included among the set of socioeconomic status hierarchies, or power rankings, because it is closely linked to the acquisition of _____ and _____ in modern societies.

18. Generally the term _____ refers to the ability to lead a healthy, happy, and prosperous existence.

19. Overall, the _____ ethnic group still tends to dominate the top of the economic power structure in Canada. Two groups which historically have ranked consistently low in the stratification system are the _____ and _____.

20. Some have suggested that the extent and pervasiveness of female subordination in the stratification system is so great that the position of women is not unlike that of a _____.

Answers

KEY TERMS AND DEFINITIONS

1. class
2. proletariat
3. status set
4. class, status, party
5. intergenerational mobility
6. vertical mobility
7. achieved status
8. class in itself
9. social differentiation
10. status hierarchy
11. horizontal mobility
12. status
13. stratum
14. bourgeoisie, petite bourgeoisie
15. institutionalized power
16. status inconsistency
17. ascribed status
18. intragenerational mobility
19. status consistency
20. class for itself
21. social class
22. social stratification
23. power

SELF QUIZ

1.	b	7.	c	13.	d
2.	c	8.	a	14.	b
3.	b	9.	c	15.	d
4.	b	10.	b	16.	c
5.	a	11.	e	17.	d
6.	d	12.	b	18.	b

FILL IN THE BLANKS

1. middle classes
2. 50%
3. feudal lord and serf; master and slave
4. curvilinear
5. vertical
6. class
7. Ontario, Atlantic
8. means of production
9. class in itself, class for itself
10. socialist, communism
11. consensus, individual action, pluralism
12. power, education, occupation
13. wealth
14. white collar, agriculture
15. twice
16. institutions
17. wealth, occupational status
18. life chances
19. British, French, Native peoples
20. minority group

CHAPTER 8

Race and Ethnic Relations

OBJECTIVES

1. To understand the processes involved in the formation of an immigrant community.

2. To understand what is meant by ethnic, racial, and minority groups especially in relation to the changing Canadian ethnic mosaic and to become acquainted with such issues as prejudice, discrimination, and racism.

3. To become more fully aware of the history and pattern of First Nations/European colonizer and French/English relationships.

4. To understand three interpretations of ethnic group relations — assimilationism, two-category perspectives, and pluralism — and to consider some of the implications of each for social policy.

PH/CBC VIDEO CLIP

"Davis Inlet: Moving from Misery"
Source: *CBC News in Review*
Running Time: 10:35 minutes

For centuries, the Inuit people have lived off the land in the harshest conditions imaginable. In 1967 a group of Inuit were moved to the island of Davis Inlet by the government of Newfoundland and Labrador , with promises of a better life, complete with running water and well-insulated houses. Many years and broken promises later, life for the 500 residents of Davis Inlet is miserable. This video addresses the isolation and despair of the Inuit people of Davis Inlet. It offers a troubling investigation of such issues as crowded living conditions, disease, alcohol and drug abuse, depression and suicide, particularly among the young of Davis Inlet, as well as a critical examination of the implications of relocation.

Discussion questions

1. As mentioned in Chapter 8, there is a great deal of diversity among Native individuals and communities. In fact many Native organizations have made substantial strides in dealing with the problems they face today. Comment on the social, economic, and political factors that have contributed to the despair that we have seen in Davis Inlet.

2. What are both the historical and contemporary reasons presented by the federal government's Indian Affairs Department for relocating Canadian Native peoples?

3. What are the arguments presented by the Inuit for relocation to the Labrador mainland?

4.   What sociological theoretical framework or frameworks would be useful to a discussion of the problems of suicide and drug abuse that are so prevalent in Davis Inlet?

KEY TERMS AND DEFINITIONS

1. _____: the view that ethnic diversity gradually and inevitably declines as group members are absorbed into the general population, in the process becoming more and more like the dominant group.

2. _____: the development of a full set of institutions in an ethnic community that parallel those in the larger society.

3. _____: an arbitrary social category membership which is based upon inherited physical characteristics defined as socially meaningful, such as skin colour or facial features.

4. _____: mental images that exaggerate traits believed to be typical of members of a social group.

5. _____: discrimination against members of a group that occurs as a by-product of the ordinary functioning of bureaucratic institutions, rather than as a consequence of a deliberate policy to discriminate.

6. _____: a social system of coexisting racial and ethnic groups, each of which maintains to some degree its own distinctive culture, social networks, and institutions, while participating with other racial and ethnic groups in common cultural, economic, and political institutions.

7. _____: the hierarchical ranking of ethnic populations in a society.

8. _____: the learning of the language, values, and customs of a dominant group by an ethnic group.

9. _____: the denial of opportunities, generally available to all members of society, to some people because of their membership in a social category.

10. _____: the maintenance of physical distance between ethnic or racial groups.

11. _____: a collection of individuals who share a particular trait that is defined as socially meaningful, but who may neither interact nor have anything else in common.

12. _____: the domination by a settler society of a native or indigenous population. In time, the native population suffers the erosion of its

traditional culture and usually occupies a subordinate status in the pluralist society of which it has involuntarily become a part.

13._____: a people — a collectivity of persons who share an ascribed status based upon culture, religion, national origin, or shared historical experience based upon a common ethnicity or race.

14._____: prejudging people based upon characteristics they are assumed to share as members of a social category.

15._____: the view on race relations that sees two, hierarchically ranked, separate collectivities in conflict, bound together in a relationship of dominance and subordination within a single society and culture.

16._____: sequential movement of persons from a common place of origin to a common destination, with the assistance of relatives or acquaintances already settled in the new location.

17._____: the view that ethnic diversity, stratification, and conflict remain central features of modern societies, and that race and ethnicity continue to be important aspects of individual identity and group behaviour.

18._____: the collective designation given by assimilationists to four stages in the relationship between dominant and minority groups. The stages are contact, competition, accommodation, and finally, assimilation.

19._____: a social category, usually ethnically or racially labeled, that occupies a subordinate rank in the social hierarchy.

20._____: the state of having within the self two conflicting social identities; also, the social condition of a minority group that lives on the edge of a society, not treated as a full member of that society.

21._____: acceptance of minority group by a dominant group into its intimate, primary, social relationships.

22._____: an ideology that regards racial or ethnic categories as natural genetic groupings and that attributes behavioural and psychological differences to the genetic nature of these groupings.

SELF QUIZ

1. Immigrants who receive legal guarantees of support from relatives or others in Canada are classified as

   a) independent immigrants
   b) chain migration immigrants
   c) sponsored immigrants
   d) marginal immigrants
   e) *de jure* immigrants

2. One factor in the development of a strong sense of solidarity, ethnic identity, and a wide range of institutions is

   a) cultural universals combined with minority group status
   b) the size of the ethnic population
   c) whether the individuals share similar values and beliefs
   d) the difference between achieved and ascribed status
   e) the experience of three solitudes

3. Weber and Barth both suggested that ethnicity has four major dimensions. Which of the following fits into their theoretical perspective?

   a) an achieved status
   b) a subculture
   c) an ascribed status
   d) a and b
   e) b and c

4. An important feature of an ethnic group as a form of social organization is that it

   a) has acculturated
   b) is fully isolated from the mainstream of society
   c) has boundaries
   d) lacks institutional completeness
   e) has assimilated into the mainstream of society

5. A 1990 survey by Decima found that _____ percent of Canadians agreed that "all races are created equal"

   a) 90
   b) 70
   c) 50
   d) 30
   e) 10

6. The term ethnogenesis refers to

   a) intense, informal interaction and communication among persons of the same ethnicity
   b) marriage within one's own ethnic group
   c) an ethnic group occupying an elite or privileged status
   d) the forcing of a common label and identity upon a group
   e) the passing on of genetic characteristics to one's ethnic group

7.   The unemployment rate for First Nations people living off reserve is roughly
      _____ the rate for the rest of Canada.

      a)   equal to
      b)   double
      c)   triple
      d)   ten times
      e)   one half

8.   Affirmative action targets include all of the following except

      a)   women
      b)   the disabled
      c)   blacks in Nova Scotia
      d)   French Canadians
      e)   First Nations

9.   Dominant groups frequently control and restrict the economic, social, and political
      participation of minorities by means of

      a)   expulsion
      b)   annihilation
      c)   discrimination
      d)   exploitation
      e)   disruption

10.   Which of the following statements is true?

      a)   *de jure* discrimination is more frequent than *de facto* discrimination
      b)   discriminatory behaviour is caused by prejudiced attitudes
      c)   victims of prejudice usually bring it on themselves
      d)   a prejudiced person may not discriminate and a person may discriminate yet not
            be prejudiced
      e)   a and b only

11.   Under the terms of the Indian Act, special status is conferred upon

      a)   the Métis
      b)   British Columbia and Manitoba Indians
      c)   the Inuit
      d)   registered Indians
      e)   a and c only

12.   The erosion of French language and culture in Canada has many complex sources.
      A main one is

      a)   the recent increase in Quebec's death rate
      b)   the fact that English-speaking immigrants to Canada far outnumber French-
            speaking immigrants
      c)   the 1977 language legislation which specified that the language of Quebec's
            French majority shall be the official language of Quebec
      d)   the victory of the Federal Progressive Conservatives in the 1980s
      e)   the economic recession of the 1990s

13.   Post World War II immigration in Canada is marked by its

      a)   ethnic networks

b) institutional completeness
c) ethnic diversity
d) tendency toward cultural assimilation
e) segregation of ethnic groups

14. Who is most likely to suffer marginality?

a) a majority member who is increasingly outnumbered by minorities
b) people who assimilate
c) an immigrant
d) colonists
e) a and d

15. Endogamy is probably most important for which group below?

a) Jews
b) Italians
c) Germans
d) Ukrainians
e) it is equally important to all groups listed

FILL IN THE BLANKS

1. Recent data suggest that almost _____ percent of all Canadians came from backgrounds other than British or French.

2. *Nunavut* means _____ in Inuktitut.

3. Many observers predict not a bilingual Canada but a Canada of _____ solitudes.

4. In the media minorities are defined as _____, in terms of race-role stereotyping, as a social problem, and as _____.

5. Pluralist societies in which peoples of various cultural, religious, or racial backgrounds live side by side within a single, social, economic, and political system exist as a consequence of the historical processes of _____, conquest, and _____.

6. A social attribute such as ethnicity, which is acquired from one's parents and other ancestors, and that is conferred at birth, is referred to as an _____.

7. A growing body of research suggests that _____ is more salient than ethnic origin in accounting for differences in occupational status and income.

8. The critical factor in the maintenance of ethnic group boundaries is _____, that is, marriage within one's own ethnic group.

9.   The Charter of the French Language is better known as _____.

10.   After the British and the French, the next largest group in Canada are the _____.

11.   The two racial/ethnic groups in Toronto whose males experienced significantly lower incomes than the majority are the _____ and _____.

12.   The _____ are those people descended from marriages between Indian women and early European settlers.

13.   _____ is a system that is democratic for the master race but tyrannical for subordinate groups.

14.   By setting a universalistic rule that all guards must weigh at least 150 pounds, a security firm may effectively be practicing _____.

15.   In intergroup relations, exaggerated mental images of groups are called _____, while the attitudes associated with them are called _____, and the behaviour sometimes associated with them is called discrimination.

16.   The _____ (1763) transferred virtually all Canadian lands under French control to the British.

17.   The pattern of French settlement which entailed the granting of lands by the French crown to landowners who declared themselves vassals to the crown is known as the _____.

18.   Columbus' calling the Native peoples of Canada "Indians" is an example of _____.

19.   The era of the _____ immigrant was a brief one in Canada, for the predominant pattern of immigrant settlement has always been urban.

20.   The perspective which generally assumes that it is only through individual achievement that upward mobility in the social hierarchy can occur, and also argues that maintaining ethnic culture and language will hinder upward mobility, is called _____.

Answers

KEY TERMS AND DEFINITIONS

1. assimilationism
2. institutional completeness
3. race
4. stereotypes
5. systemic or institutionalized discrimination
6. pluralistic society
7. vertical mosaic
8. acculturation
9. discrimination
10. segregation
11. social category
12. colonialism
13. ethnic group
14. prejudice
15. two-category perspectives
16. chain migration
17. pluralism
18. race relations cycle
19. minority group
20. marginality
21. structural assimilation
22. racism

SELF QUIZ

1. c
2. b
3. e
4. c
5. a
6. d
7. c
8. d
9. c
10. d
11. d
12. b
13. c
14. c
15. a

FILL IN THE BLANKS

1. 50
2. our land
3. two unilingual
4. invisible, amusement
5. colonialism, migration
6. ascribed status
7. race
8. endogamy
9. Bill 101
10. Germans
11. Chinese and West Indians
12. Métis
13. Herrenvolk democracy
14. institutionalized discrimination
15. stereotypes, prejudice
16. Treaty of Paris
17. seigneurial system
18. ethnogenesis
19. family
20. assimilationism

CHAPTER 9

Families

OBJECTIVES

1. To learn terms such as nuclear family, consanguine family, exogamy, polygamy, matriarchal, and patrilocal, to name a few, which reflect the variety of kinship and family forms.

2. To be aware of the differences in family patterns across societies.

3. To understand two theoretical perspectives concerning changes in family structure: functionalism and a more conflict position.

4. To understand the life cycle of the family, from socialization for marriage, to childbearing and child-rearing.

5. To understand the changing role of the family both in society and in the lives of individuals.

KEY TERMS AND DEFINITIONS

1. _____: the lesser power of a woman in marriage partly arising from her being younger than her husband.

2. _____: the emotional dimension of marriage, including gratification, companionship, and empathy.

3. _____: marriage of persons with similar physical, psychological, or social characteristics. This is the tendency for like to marry like.

4. _____: a commitment and an ongoing exchange. The commitment can include legal or contractual elements, as well as social pressures against dissolution. The arrangement includes both instrumental and expressive exchanges.

5. _____: a nuclear family consisting of partners who are not legally married, with or without children.

6. _____: the task-oriented dimension of marriage, including earning a living, spending money, and maintaining a household.

7. There is a variety of marital structures: _____ marriage in which the husband owns his wife; _____ marriage in which the wife finds meaning in life through her husband; _____ marriage in which the wife is employed, but her

job and income are less important than her husband's; and finally _____ marriage in which both spouses are equally committed to marriage and a career.

8.　　　　　　　There are a variety of premarital sexual standards: the _____ standard allows no premarital sex; the _____ standard allows it for men only; the _____ standard permits premarital sex for persons if there is a strong personal commitment; and the _____ standard approves of it for both men and women, even without love.

9. _____: descent traced unilaterally through the male line; a child is related only to the father's relatives.

10. _____: one woman married to two or more men; wife-sharing.

11. _____: a family consisting of one parent and one or more children.

12. _____: the norm that marriage partners must be chosen from outside a defined group.

13. _____: marriage involving two or more men and two or more women.

14. _____: the residence pattern of couples who reside alone.

15. _____: a marriage relationship in which there is equal power of wife and husband.

16. _____: a family that includes more than spouses and unmarried children (e.g., grandparents, married children, other relatives) living in the same residence.

17. _____: the norm that marriage partners must be members of the same group.

18. _____: couple takes up residence with the wife's parents.

19. _____: marriage involving more than two partners.

20. _____: people related by blood or marriage.

21. _____: males are the formal head and ruling power in the families.

22. _____: descent that follows both the male and female lines; a child is related to relatives of both parents.

23._____: a family organization in which the primary emphasis is on biological relatedness (e.g., parents and children or brothers and sisters), rather than on the spousal relationship.

24._____: marriage involving only two partners.

25._____: society in which females are the formal head and ruling power in the families.

26._____: two or more people related by blood, marriage, or adoption and residing together.

27._____: one man married to two or more women; husband-sharing.

28._____: descent traced unilaterally through the female line; a child is related only to the mother's relatives.

29._____: couple takes up residence with the husband's parents.

30._____: a family that includes only spouses and any unmarried children.

31._____: marriage between two people who are dissimilar in some important regard, such as religion, ethnic background, social class, personality, or age.

32._____: a nuclear family that includes children from more than one marriage or union.

33._____: a nuclear family with children from a prior union of one of the spouses.

SELF QUIZ

1.   Cohabitation is generally

   a)   patriarchal
   b)   matriarchal
   c)   polygynous
   d)   neolocal
   e)   hedonistic

2.   For a unit to be called a family, the people involved must

   a)   customarily live in the same dwelling
   b)   be related
   c)   be related and customarily live in the same dwelling
   d)   be related by marriage or common-law union
   e)   include at least one person of each sex

3. From anthropological data gathered in various societies it is clear that only two types of marriage have been found with any frequency. They are

    a) group marriage and polygyny
    b) polygamy and monogamy
    c) monogamy and group marriage
    d) polygyny and polyandry
    e) monogamy and polygyny

4. In tribal societies

    a) the nuclear family is generally paramount
    b) reproduction is at a premium
    c) the consanguine family is generally paramount
    d) children are often spoiled
    e) b and c

5. Which of the following practices is the most uniform across societies?

    a) acceptance of extra-marital intercourse
    b) the incest taboo
    c) discouragement of premarital intercourse
    d) low premium on marriage
    e) endogamy

6. Which perspective looks at the family as one of the institutions of society and concentrates on instrumental exchanges?

    a) symbolic interactionism
    b) feminism
    c) functionalism
    d) social psychology
    e) conflict theory

7. What factor(s) most helped to decrease or change the functions previously performed by families?

    a) a reduced influence of religion and a decline in the birth rate
    b) industrialization
    c) the women's liberation movement and reactions to it
    d) the increase in the number of divorces
    e) a and d

8. The discussion about expressive exchanges concluded that

    a) the family has maintained most of its economic, political, and religious functions
    b) the family has become more important as a source of emotional gratification for individuals
    c) families are more likely to stay together today than previously because they are a source of emotional gratification for individuals
    d) families are now quicker to break apart when individual members do not find a particular arrangement to be gratifying, a luxury they could not afford as providers of instrumental needs
    e) b and d

9.   Which of the following statements is true?

   a)   in some hunting and gathering societies, the sexes were considerably more equal than they are today
   b)   the relative status of men and women in society has little to do with their roles in economic production
   c)   early industrialism allowed the sexes to become considerably more equal than they were previously
   d)   cultural norms have little if any impact on the roles of men and women; economics is the main factor
   e)   none of the above

10.   Which standard of premarital sexuality received the greatest support among post-secondary students?

   a)   love
   b)   abstinence
   c)   double
   d)   fun
   e)   all standards were equally supported

11.   Most research on mate selection supports the following conclusion: mate selection or choice of marital partner tends to be

   a)   homogamous
   b)   heterogamous
   c)   polygynous
   d)   b and c
   e)   a and c

12.   Which group is least likely to practice religious endogamy?

   a)   Roman Catholics
   b)   Jews
   c)   Anglicans
   d)   Pentecostals
   e)   a to d are equally likely to do so

13.   Among persons getting married in any year, probably close to _____ were married previously.

   a)   2%
   b)   10%
   c)   25%
   d)   50%
   e)   75%

14.   Which of the following is (are) false?

   a)   because of the burdens of childrearing, marriages involving children have a higher divorce rate than childless unions
   b)   the younger the age at marriage, the greater the incidence of divorce
   c)   because they have been hurt once already, people entering second marriages have a lower divorce rate than those entering first marriages
   d)   women in senior-partner junior-partner marriages are more likely to divorce than those in head-complement
   e)   a and c

15. Which of the following statements is true?
    a) in the future, the institution of marriage may no longer exist
    b) the proportion of married people among the adult population is almost as high as ever
    c) childless couples will be the norm in the future
    d) in most marriages, men and women are equal partners
    e) a and c

FILL IN THE BLANKS

1. Marriages preceded by cohabitation have _____ rates of dissolution than those in which the couple do not live together before marriage.

2. Persons who customarily maintain a common residence but are not related form a _____ and not a family.

3. Murdock's research discovered that although polygyny is accepted in many societies, in practice the majority of marriages in these societies are

    _____.

4. The regulation of sexual behaviour outside of marriage shows variability across societies. Still, Murdock found that the majority of societies _____ premarital intercourse.

5. Most individuals are motivated to marry and they have the potential ability. What they lack is _____.

6. Concerning uniformity in family structure across societies, in most societies there is a high premium on _____. Another feature that is almost uniform is the incest taboo. Finally, the importance of _____ is found in most societies.

7. The theoretical perspective which assumes that families or kin groups in nonindustrial settings have a far wider range of tasks to perform than they do in industrial society is known as _____.

8. Some functionalist researchers have argued that industrialization brought about a change from an _____ family to a _____ family structure but the author of the chapter does not accept this argument.

9. Today the functions of the family are largely limited to procreation, the raising of children and to _____.

10. Nonindustrial societies were held together by _____, that is, by the sense of identity people had with their communities. In the industrial world,

societies are held together by _____, a division of labour that allows individuals to profit from the specialized abilities of others.

11. Wealthier men are more likely than poorer men to marry. Are wealthier women more, less, or equally likely to marry than poorer women? _____

12. From a Marxist point of view, males and females may be seen as _____, each with distinctive roles to play in the productive process.

13. *Eros* and *agape* are forms of _____.

14. Lupri and Mills analyzed time budgets of several hundred working couples in Calgary and concluded that, especially in families with _____, the wife ends up with a greater share of the housework.

15. In everyday conversations about mate selection, two contradictory principles often emerge: "opposites attract" and "like marries like." Which principle receives considerably more support? _____

16. The potentially happy time period in a family that occurs after children have moved away is called the _____.

17. Relative power of spouses, although very difficult to measure, is another important aspect of marital interactions. It has been found that the power of the wife is _____ if she is at home with young children, and _____ when she is working.

18. Couples with young children at home are more likely to be _____ than are childless couples or those whose children have left home.

ANSWERS

KEY TERMS AND DEFINITIONS

1. mating gradient
2. expressive exchanges
3. homogamy
4. marriage
5. common-law union
6. instrumental exchanges

7. owner-property; head-complement; senior-partner junior- partner; equal partners
8. abstinence; double; love; fun
9. patrilineal
10. polyandry
11. single parent family

12. exogamy
13. group marriage
14. neolocal
15. equalitarian
16. extended family
17. endogamy
18. matrilocal
19. polygamy
20. kin
21. patriarchal
22. bilateral

23. consanguine family
24. monogamy
25. matriarchal
26. family
27. polygyny
28. matrilineal
29. patrilocal
30. nuclear family
31. heterogamy
32. blended family
33. reconstituted family

SELF QUIZ

1. d
2. c
3. e
4. e
5. b
6. c

7. b
8. e
9. a
10. a
11. a
12. c

13. d
14. c
15. e
16. b

FILL IN THE BLANKS

1. higher
2. household
3. monogamous
4. tolerate
5. knowledge of what is expected
6. marriage, inheritance
7. functionalism
8. extended, nuclear
9. meeting the emotional needs of family members
10. mechanical solidarity, organic solidarity
11. less
12. social classes
13. love
14. children
15. like marries like
16. empty nest
17. lowest, highest
18. dissatisfied

CHAPTER 10

Religion

OBJECTIVES

1.   To understand Durkheim's views on the causes, consequences, and functions of religion.

2.   To understand Weber's analysis of religion and social change with specific emphasis on the Protestant ethic and its relation to the growth of capitalism.

3.   To be able to compare and contrast different types of religious organizations including: sect, church, denomination, ecclesia, and cult.

4.   To understand Marx's view of religion as ideology.

5.   To understand the secularization of religion in modern times with an emphasis on the situation in Canada.

6.   To be aware of the new religious movements and the functions they serve.

KEY TERMS AND DEFINITIONS

1. The social role of religion in traditional society includes five functions:

a) _____: to give meaning to mundane events.

b) _____: to keep members of a society participating in common activities beneficial to that society.

c) _____: to explain seemingly inexplicable natural phenomena and a society's social organization to its members.

d) _____: to order and control the daily activities and events of believers.

e) _____: to mirror in dramatic, artistic, and symbolic form the elements of social organization in a society.

2. _____   a religious attitude that rejects the world as illusion and offers salvation through detachment from the physical world.

3. _____: an attitude of self-denial in favor of economic gain.

4. _____: the common beliefs and rituals of a political community that interpret political activity in religious or quasi-religious terms.

5. _____: those objects and activities set apart by society and treated with awe and respect.

6. _____: the process by which traditional religious beliefs and rituals lose their hold on society and other institutions take over their functions.

7. _____: competing church-like religious organizations.

8. _____: a directive for inner-worldly asceticism attributed by Weber to early Protestant groups.

9. _____: the parallel development of two distinct social phenomena that serve to reinforce each other.

10. _____: a type of non-established religious group characterized by voluntary membership, a radical social outlook, and rigorous demands.

11. _____: a purpose in life. In a religious context it is a belief that people are born with certain abilities in order to fulfill God's will on earth through their life's work.

12. _____: a relatively well-articulated statement of beliefs and objectives that can be used to justify patterns of conduct, especially worldly activities; used by Marx to describe religion.

13. _____: Durkheim's term for the religion of the future that he believed would hold the idealized human individual as sacred.

14. _____: those objects and activities seen by a society as devoid of supernatural power or significance, of concern only to the individual.

15. _____: another term for church used by sociologists to describe the dominating or sole religious order of a society, as opposed to denomination.

16. _____: the process of organizational change whereby for purposes of group survival: 1) authority is transferred from a personal charismatic leader to non-charismatic officials; 2) spontaneous patterns of group organization become fixed and ritualized; and 3) the members and leaders experience reinvolvement with the secular world.

17. _____: a type of non-established religious organization characterized by voluntary membership. It is often highly intellectual and features a loosely knit organization that makes few claims on members.

18. _____: according to Weber, a way of giving meaning to one's existence, a way of escaping pain and suffering.

19._____: any culturally transmitted system of beliefs and rituals to which people orient themselves in order to understand their world with reference to what they regard as sacred reality.

20._____: a religious attitude that offers salvation through self-discipline and accepts the world as an arena for religious activity.

21._____: the belief that an individual's spiritual salvation is determined before birth by divine plan.

22._____: the process by which the world is perceived as losing its magical, religious, and nonrational attributes.

23._____: a type of established religious organization usually characterized by membership by birth. It often represents the only religion of a given society.

24._____: the recognition and acceptance of authoritative claims based not on traditions, rational argument, or accepted procedures, but on the person or group of persons and their personal messages.

25._____: Bibby's idea that religious beliefs and services are increasingly treated by people as items to be chosen or discarded at will.

26._____: a generic term used to describe a range of recent religious groups, typically of the cult or sect variety.

SELF QUIZ

1.   Canadian Judaism was described as having aspects of:
   a)   civil religion
   b)   a cult but not a sect
   c)   consumer religion
   d)   a and c
   e)   a, b, and c

2.   Baptism, communion, marriage, and burial were each steps that transformed and defined the individual's relationship to the social group among the parishioners of St. Denis. According to Durkheim, which function of religion do these events serve?
   a)   to regulate
   b)   to represent
   c)   to interpret
   d)   to integrate
   e)   to empower

3.   In his discussion of the Arunta, Durkheim noted how all aspects of their lives were divided into two categories. Those activities or things that individuals shared with the group as a whole he labelled

a) profane
b) totems
c) sacred
d) rituals
e) emblems

4. The idea that salvation lies in continuing to live in the world and carefully disciplining the body and the senses so as to avoid the excess of pain or pleasure, is part of

a) Hindu belief
b) other-worldly mysticism
c) inner-worldly asceticism
d) the capitalist tradition
e) predestination

5. According to Weber, the spirit of capitalism was nourished by a combination of

a) the accumulation of wealth and hedonism
b) self-denial and the accumulation of wealth
c) religious dogma and rational thinking
d) the routinization of charisma and industrialization
e) a and d

6. The process that involves the compromise by religious leaders of their religious ideals with worldly concerns, even to the extent that their religions come to represent the wealth and power of the world, is known as

a) false consciousness
b) the Protestant ethic
c) other-worldly mysticism
d) collective effervescence
e) the routinization of charisma

7. The Jehovah's Witnesses are probably closest to which type of religious organization?

a) church
b) cult
c) sect
d) denomination
e) ecclesia

8. Which of the following is true?

a) denominations very often become sects
b) cults have been known to become sects
c) ecclesia never become denominations
d) sects often become denominations
e) b and d

9.   The Sunday Trading Bill, while supposedly protecting religious values, affected mainly the poorer classes. Which theorist(s) made this point?

a)   Weber
b)   Marx
c)   Durkheim
d)   Bibby
e)   Durkheim and Marx

10. Marx's image of religion was one of "flowers on the chains" and seems best suited for societies dominated by .

a)   socialism
b)   denominations
c)   ecclesia
d)   communism
e)   sectarian religions

11. Which of the following seems to be associated with secularization?

a)   urbanization
b)   mechanical solidarity and lack of specialization
c)   industrialization
d)   increased church attendance
e)   a and c

12. An Arunta man could not marry his _____, evidence in support of Durkheim's explanation of totemism.

a)   father's brother's daughter
b)   mother's brother's daughter
c)   mother's sister's daughter
d)   neighbor
e)   none of the above; there were no rules concerning exogamy among the Arunta

13. What seems to accompany industrialization and most sociologists agree that is a gradual but continual process in technological societies?

a)   cult of man
b)   disenchantment of the world
c)   secularization
d)   other worldly mysticism
e)   inner worldly asceticism

14. Various explanations have been given by sociologists for the growth and interest in new religious movements. Which of the following is not an explanation?

a)   new religious movements fulfill the expressive and empowering functions which remain the domain of religion
b)   new religious movements go against the trend, avoiding charismatic leaders
c)   new religious movements offer guidance and an escape from moral confusion
d)   new religious movements offer magical techniques for controlling the environment
e)   new religious movements focus not so much on group life but on self realization

15. One alternative to traditional religion involves public ceremonies which are in fact celebrations of a way of life sacred to a national group. This alternative is known as:

    a) invisible religion
    b) consumer religion
    c) popular religion
    d) new religious movements
    e) none of the above

FILL IN THE BLANKS

1. Durkheim compared the religious experience with the experience of being in a crowd and termed the emotional and contagious aspect of crowd behaviour

   _____.

2. Durkheim saw the origin of religious experience and the source of religious power as located in the effects on individuals of the _____.

3. Students with a strong spiritual orientation are more satisfied with their lives, experience better _____ and are better able to handle _____.

4. Religions such as _____ and _____ are currently among the fastest-growing religious groups in Canada.

5. The Protestant ethic originated in the teachings of Calvin who preached the notion of predestination, that individuals at birth have been determined by God as either _____ or _____.

6. Weber argued that the combination of _____ and the _____ among the early Protestants laid the groundwork for the spirit of capitalism.

7. According to Bibby, most people accept, at least nominally, the religious affiliation of their _____.

8. Awareness of the sexist nature of much of religion is not new. In fact in 1895 Elizabeth Cady Stanton published _____.

9. Of the following religions in Canada, only _____ has generally maintained its share of membership over time: Roman Catholicism, Anglicanism, the United Church.

10. Transcendental Meditation and est are examples of the type of religious organizations called _____.

11.   The liberal agenda of several Protestant groups in western Canada, also influential in the formation of the CCF, was called _____.

12.   Heterogeneous membership, acceptance of the world, and a hired leader are characteristic of a _____.

13.   *Hockey Night in Canada* was included as a part of what was called _____ religion.

14.   The need to find a successor for a charismatic leader in a religious movement often triggers _____.

15.   To keep followers under some control, religious leaders need to appoint assistants and to tone down the emotional nature of their meetings. This is an aspect of _____.

ANSWERS

KEY TERMS AND DEFINITIONS

1.   to empower, to integrate, to interpret, to regulate, to represent
2.   other-worldly mysticism
3.   spirit of capitalism
4.   civil religion
5.   sacred
6.   secularization
7.   denominations
8.   Protestant ethic
9.   elective affinity
10.   sect
11.   calling
12.   ideology
13.   cult of man

14.   profane
15.   ecclesia
16.   routinization of charisma
17.   cult
18.   salvation
19.   religion
20.   inner-worldly asceticism
21.   predestination
22.   disenchantment of the world
23.   church
24.   charisma
25.   consumer religion
26.   new religious movements

SELF QUIZ

1.	d	6.	e	11.	e
2.	d	7.	c	12.	a
3.	c	8.	e	13.	c
4.	c	9.	b	14.	b
5.	b	10.	c	15.	e

FILL IN THE BLANKS

1. collective effervescence
2. social group
3. health both physically and emotionally, stress
4. Hinduism and Islam
5. the chosen, the damned
6. ceaseless hard work, accumulation of wealth
7. parents
8. The Woman's' Bible
9. Roman Catholicism
10. cult
11. Social Gospel
12. church
13. invisible
14. the routinization of charisma
15. the routinization of charisma

CHAPTER 11

Education

OBJECTIVES

1. To be aware of the growth of education in Canada and to understand the effects of demographic trends and increased participation rates on the most recent educational expansion.

2. To understand the three major sociological theories of educational expansion — functionalism, capital accumulation, and cultural markets — and the criticisms of each.

3. To understand the impact educational expansion has had upon equality of educational and social opportunities for social class and gender categories.

4. To become acquainted with some of the studies of school resources, especially what goes on in classrooms, and how activity there affects both learning and inequality.

5. To understand the relationship among schooling, mobility, and success and predictions about the future of schooling.

PH/CBC VIDEO CLIP

"Educating Girls"
Source: *Prime Time News*
Running Time: 9:00 minutes

Should teenage girls have their own separate classes or even their own separate schools? In recent years, several studies claim to have found a gender bias against girls in coeducational classrooms. Some educators believe the current system discourages young teenaged girls in subjects such as math and physics. *Educating Girls* examines a physics class with a difference in Calgary, Alberta. Students and teachers comment on the benefits and drawbacks to gender-specific classrooms.

Discussion questions

1. Discuss the reasons presented in the video as to why girls do not pursue an education in maths and sciences. Do you find these reasonable?

2. What are some of the differences that are presented by the teacher in Calgary in the learning approaches between boys and girls?

3. Comment on the differences you observed in the behaviours of the students in the girls-only physics class and the mixed-gender physics class.

4. What are some of your personal reflections of learning based on mixed classes or gender specific classes?

KEY TERMS AND DEFINITIONS

1. _____: a language code that is relatively informal and depends upon the listener understanding the context, and is expressed through short sentences and simple grammar; useful for communicating immediate experiences to friends and others familiar with a situation.

2. _____: an alternative to functionalism and capital accumulation theory, it stresses the competition among different types of groups for varying kinds and amounts of schooling.

3. _____: explains education in terms of what it attempts to accomplish: skill acquisition, preparation for job selection, legitimizing social position, and passing on core values, moral education, and the essentials of good citizenship.

4. _____: the theory of education that argues that capitalists use schools to defuse class antagonism and to make workers docile, cooperative employees.

5. _____: a language code that is relatively formal and does not depend on the listener knowing the speaker's situation intimately and that facilitates discussion of symbolic and conceptual issues.

6. _____: applied to education, it means that educational systems are similar in structure to society's economic mode of production. More generally, it is the Marxist view that social institutions mirror the mode of production.

SELF QUIZ

1. The main factor(s) behind the educational expansion of the 1950s and 1960s was (were)

    a) an increased participation rate
    b) the baby boom
    c) an increase in the number of women attending university
    d) an increase in part-time enrollments
    e) a and b

2. Functionalists would claim that Canada's school system was started and expanded because

    a) the achievement-oriented system was not functioning properly and there was a threat of domination from the U.S.
    b) the family was not fulfilling its role as a socializing agent
    c) it helped in the process of job selection and in the passing on of core values needed by a diverse population
    d) equality of both educational opportunity and results was the major goal in society
    e) none of the above

3. At all levels of university the smallest representation of women is found in

    a) health fields
    b) social science
    c) education
    d) engineering
    e) math and sciences

4. An alternative to functionalist thought is capital accumulation theory. From this perspective schools were started

    a) in response to the needs of society
    b) to allow all to accumulate capital for investment
    c) to discourage the accumulation of material wealth
    d) to meet the needs of capitalism and to serve as a key component of worker control
    e) to integrate immigrants into society

5. The perspective called cultural market theory is pluralist and draws its major arguments from the writings of

    a) Marx
    b) Durkheim
    c) Weber
    d) Mead
    e) Porter

6. A _____ may be more consistent with women's preferred ways of knowing.

    a) connected teaching model
    b) authoritarian banking model
    c) adversarial doubting model
    d) process model
    e) b and c

7. Which group probably benefited most from the expansion of universities?

    a) the upper class
    b) the working class
    c) men
    d) the middle class
    e) all groups benefited equally

8.   Educational reforms of the 1950s to 1970s favored

    a)   math over English
    b)   English over math
    c)   greater gender equality
    d)   increasing student autonomy
    e)   elaborate codes

9.   The line between education and work is less distinct in Canada than elsewhere. Evidence for this is that

    a)   corporations are now running schools
    b)   university education has almost no effect on earnings
    c)   we enter and reenter both educational institutions and the labour market
    d)   it has widespread apprenticeship programs
    e)   education is a provincial responsibility

10.   A British study by Wells concluded that the factor most strongly related to student educational achievement at age ten is

    a)   social class
    b)   the students' final grades from the previous year
    c)   where the students sat in the classroom and whether their teachers liked them
    d)   literacy
    e)   none of the above

11.   Bernstein argued that social class affects peoples' language skills and the way they articulate their thoughts. Working-class people are more likely to rely on

    a)   an ethnocentric language
    b)   a restricted code
    c)   an activity code
    d)   linguistic relativism
    e)   an elaborated code

12.   Which of the following statements is true concerning the relationship between education and status attainment?

    a)   status attainment may be affected more by economic and family factors than by educational factors alone
    b)   there is little relationship because most students do not really believe in the value of higher education
    c)   in Canada the lines between school and work are more distinct than those in Great Britain
    d)   schooling is three times more important in determining occupational attainment than is family background
    e)   c and d

FILL IN THE BLANKS

1.   Today, one out of every _____ people in Canada is in school in one capacity or another.

2.   _____ have been characterized as a proletarian alternative to the university.

3.   According to Richer the _____ curriculum teaches children to value competition, private property, work over play, and submission to authority.

4.   Including Latin, philosophy, and classics as parts of the curriculum is best explained by the _____ theory.

5.   To capital accumulation theorists, schools were started by employers as one way of rendering harmless the potentially explosive _____ antagonisms that accompanied the spread of capitalism in the form of the factory system.

6.   Both functionalism and capital accumulation theories tend to see educational change as essentially _____.

7.   In the case of modern schooling, _____ such as degrees, diplomas, and certificates — not necessarily education or training in themselves — are the key goods sought.

8.   In Canada's competitive and achievement-oriented school system, inequality is a way of life. Traditionally, the key issue was not equality of results but equality of _____.

9.   While children tend to have symbolic understandings, schools tend to stress academic or _____ understanding.

10.   Girls are less likely than boys to take and to do well in secondary school math and science courses, with the exception of the subject of _____.

11.   Approximately _____ percent of all 14- to 17-year-olds attend school.

12.   The word school comes from the Greek word for _____, a derivation reflecting both the scarcity of schools and the privileged background of those who attended them.

13.   _____, allocating secondary students to different levels on the basis of perceived ability and vocational objectives, is common in Canada. Large-scale studies of it have not supported its critics.

14. Studies of the German education system would suggest that _____ programs might reduce the drop out rate. A downside is that they are of more benefit to boys than girls.

15. The future of Canadian education will include greater decentralization and more alternatives including a proliferation of programs recognizing the needs of

_____.

ANSWERS

KEY TERMS AND DEFINITIONS

1. restricted code
2. cultural markets theory
3. functional theory of education

4. capital accumulation theory
5. elaborated code
6. correspondence principle

SELF QUIZ

1. e
2. c
3. d
4. d

5. c
6. a
7. d
8. d

9. e
10. d
11. b
12. a

FILL IN THE BLANKS

1. three
2. community colleges
3. hidden
4. cultural markets
5. class
6. rational
7. credentials
8. opportunity
9. disciplinary
10. biology
11. 90

12. leisure
13. streaming
14. apprenticeship
15. special groups

CHAPTER 12

State and Politics

OBJECTIVES

1. To understand three general theoretical perspectives on the state: pluralist, elitist, and Marxist, including recent challenges to the last.

2. To learn what Hegel had to say about the state, especially about civil society and the universal class.

3. To understand the welfare state and current neoconservative challenges to it in Canada.

4. To be aware of the crisis of Canadian federalism.

5. To know about the role of class and gender in politics in Canada.

KEY TERMS AND DEFINITIONS

1. _____: Pareto's conception that the decline of one elite prepares the way for domination of another. Lions seize power, become foxes, and are in turn replaced by new lions.

2. _____: the idea that a country's economic development is dependent upon decisions and policies made elsewhere.

3. _____: Michel's idea that the leadership of democratically run organizations becomes elitist and tends to seek power for its own ends.

4. _____: Mills' concept for the combination of business, political, and military leaders he saw as ruling the United States.

5. _____: the relationships of power and prestige between nation-states that determine a nation's legitimacy at home.

6. _____: Hegel's notion of the state that unites the principle of the family with the idea of civil society.

7. _____: the notion that power in all forms of society is inevitably held by a small ruling group.

8. _____: Hegel's class of government or state-sector workers.

9. _____: an organization that successfully claims a monopoly on the legitimate use of force within a territory.

10._____: government characterized by free elections, contested by competing political parties and guaranteed by effective civil liberties.

11._____: Hegel's market system of industry and exchange; its principle is individual self-interest and personal gain.

12._____: the view that power in modern society is shared among competing interest groups.

13._____: according to Weber, power that is seen as legitimate by those subjected to it.

14._____: the ability to command resources, both material and human; the possibility of imposing one's will upon the behaviour of others.

15._____: Innis' view that Canada's economic well-being is heavily dependent upon the export of staples or raw materials. This in turn compromises Canadian political sovereignty.

16._____: the interdisciplinary blend of economics, political science, history, and sociology. It argues that economics makes sense only within the framework of politics and history.

17._____: the political party or group which controls the state

18._____: the view that government's role in the economy and society should be severely restricted. It generally argues for free trade, zero inflation, deficit reduction, shifting the tax burden away from corporations and the rich, and reducing the welfare state.

19._____: one that protects citizens from the excesses of market forces and treats every person equally.

SELF QUIZ

1. According to Hegel the historical order in the western world was

   a) state, socialism, communism
   b) family, state, civil society
   c) state, family, civil society
   d) family, civil society, state
   e) civil society, state, family

2. Which of the following statements is (are) part of the elitist perspective?

   a) in all liberal democracies there is a broad consensus of values and beliefs
   b) the decline of one ruling group merely prepares the way for the domination of another
   c) the iron law of oligarchy
   d) the business class will merge into the universal class
   e) b and c

3. Porter's book on the role of elites in Canadian society, *The Vertical Mosaic*, found that

   a) Canada is an open society whose citizens enjoy equal opportunities to share its positions of privilege and power
   b) Canada is divided into a pluralist system of competing elites
   c) there can be consensus in society even if people are divided by class relationships of ownership and non-ownership of the means of production
   d) the economic elite and the political elite are virtually indistinguishable
   e) none of the above

4. The universal class would include

   a) architects
   b) teachers
   c) small business people
   d) corporate executives
   e) c and d

5. In Hegelian terms, which of the following best represents the concept of civil society?

   a) Canada
   b) the former USSR
   c) the United States
   d) Great Britain
   e) there are no existing examples of civil society; it is only an ideal

6. Marx believed that capitalist society ultimately would consist of only capitalists and workers, whereas Hegel insisted that the development of the modern state would coincide with the growth of the

   a) business class
   b) rational class
   c) civil class
   d) industrial class
   e) universal class

7. International exports, dependency relations, and metropolitan powers are each a part of _____ theory.

   a) corporatist
   b) functionalist
   c) reproductive labour
   d) welfare state
   e) staples

8. Child labour is one of the prices of

   a) the welfare state
   b) structural Marxism
   c) globalization
   d) postmodernism
   e) zero inflation

9. Historically, which of the following was probably most likely to be elected to Canada's Parliament?

   a) a female doctor
   b) a male lawyer
   c) a worker with a Grade 12 education (as an NDP)
   d) an immigrant
   e) b and c

10. Which of the following statements is true?

    a) The working class in Canada is more likely to vote NDP than Liberal or Conservative.
    b) Catholics are generally more likely to vote Conservative than Liberal.
    c) Protestants are generally more likely to vote Liberal than Conservative or NDP.
    d) The working class in Canada is more likely to vote Liberal or Conservative than NDP.
    e) b and c only

FILL IN THE BLANKS

1. Pluralists argue that modern democratic societies are led by _____ groups, each having the power to veto proposed policies if they are considered harmful to its position.

2. A key assumption of the pluralist model is that in all liberal democracies there is a broad _____.

3. According to Marx, the class that controls the _____ also rules the state.

4. Kopinak's study found that among elected officials, women's policies generally reflect a _____ orientation while men's have a _____ orientation.

5. A major problem for Canadian federalism is section 33 of the Charter, the _____ clause.

6. According to _____, culture rather than economics is the dominant paradigm. Its proponents are profoundly suspicious of the state.

7. Hegel divided society into three parts: _____, _____, and _____.

8. The power of the universal class rests not on the ownership of property but in its _____.

9. Those signs which include a red circle and slash prohibiting various things are called _____.

10. Public adulation and Trudeau's personality are most relevant to Weber's _____ type of authority.

11. Women MPs are even more likely than men to come from _____ backgrounds.

12. The Reform Party and the National Action Committee did agree on the 1992 Referendum and voted on the _____ side.

13. Maquiladores are the tax free manufacturing zones which pay low wages and are found in _____.

14. _____ authority is rooted in time-honored attitudes and practices.

15. Even though there are increasing numbers of women in Parliament, "women's" issues such as day care often get shunted aside in favor of concerns for the _____.

ANSWERS

KEY TERMS AND DEFINITIONS

1. circulation of elites
2. dependency theory
3. iron law of oligarchy
4. power elite
5. geopolitics
6. ideal state
7. elitism
8. universal class
9. state
10. liberal democracy
11. civil society
12. pluralism
13. authority
14. power
15. staples approach
16. political economy
17. government
18. neoconservatism
19. welfare state

SELF QUIZ

1. e
2. e
3. b
4. b
5. c
6. e
7. e
8. c
9. b
10. d

FILL IN THE BLANKS

1. competing interest
2. consensus on values and beliefs
3. economy
4. community, business
5. notwithstanding
6. postmodernism
7. the family, civil society, the state
8. superior knowledge
9. official graffiti
10. charismatic
11. wealthy
12. No
13. Mexico
14. Traditional
15. budget deficit

CHAPTER 13

Formal Organizations and Work

OBJECTIVES

1. To understand what is meant by organization and differentiate among the concepts of formal organization, informal organization, and bureaucracy.

2. To understand the classical theoretical perspectives on formal organization including those of Durkheim, Cooley, Weber, Michels, and Marx. Scientific management and the human relations school are also presented.

3. To understand the strengths and weaknesses of modern theoretical perspectives on formal organization: the structuralist approach, negotiated order, ethnomethodology, and new industrial sociology.

4. To be aware of the principles of Japanese management styles especially as they are applied in Canada.

PH/CBC VIDEO CLIP

"Bell Pak"
Source: Prime Time News
Running Time: 9:45

As companies become more efficient and employees demand more flexibility in their working hours, a four-day work week has become the norm in some businesses. *Bell Pak* illustrates how a four-day work week has arrived as both a concept and as a fact of life for many working Canadians as an antidote to cutbacks, unemployment, layoffs, and high operating costs of business. Yet, while some people are willing to share their work and many appreciate their new-found free time, still others within this tough economy demand all the days of work they can obtain. Frank Reid of the Centre for Industrial Relations at the University of Toronto and Ruth Rose, an economist with the University of Quebec at Montreal, join Pamela Wallin in a candid discussion about the fundamental issue of whether the four-day work week is really just a short-term scheme to save some jobs or whether it could be part of a long-term plan to effectively create work in a discouraging economy.

Discussion questions

1. A capitalist society encourages the accumulation of private property and defines a profit-minded orientation as natural and simply a matter of "doing business." A four-day work week, however, means a seven and one-half percent pay cut and additional compulsory days off without pay for some employees of Bell Canada. Does a four-day work week, as outlined by the example at Bell Canada, achieve capitalist values? Explain.

2. How is it demonstrated in this video that a four-day work week may alleviate some of the problems of unemployment in Canada?

3.   How could you apply some of the theoretical concepts expanded on in this chapter to the issue of unemployment and the four-day work week?

4.   What do you think of the suggestion made in the video that "All of us who work for a living are going to have to re-evaluate time rather than money as life's reward. But if Bell's experience is anything to go by, that may not be such a big leap"?

5.   What are some of your personal thoughts on the advantages and disadvantages of a four-day work week, keeping in mind the objectives of business managers as well as employees?

KEY TERMS AND DEFINITIONS

1. _____: the study of formal organization in which the Marxian concept of alienation remains central. It sees the history of formal organization as the theory of capitalist control of workers and their subsequent alienation.

2. _____: a research strategy that extracts the most prominent or essential features of a social phenomenon. In its pure or abstract form it is not found in reality, since no one individual case perfectly embodies all essential features.

3. _____: Michels' idea that the leadership of even democratically run organizations becomes elitist and seeks power for its own ends.

4. _____: the theory of organizations stressing economic needs of individuals and workplace organization. Efficiency is believed to result from providing proper economic incentives to workers.

5. _____: an interrelated set of occupational roles or other specializations within a group or society.

6. _____: the theory of formal organizations that focuses upon the process by which an organization is socially constructed, through conflicts of interest, dialogue, and regular negotiation on the part of its participants.

7. _____: the idea that society is held together by a rational agreement to cooperate. This agreement prevents the chaos of war of all against all.

8. _____: the approach to studying organizations that stresses informal work practices and that holds that workers are motivated more by social than by economic rewards.

9. _____: according to Weber, the authority that rests on a belief in rules and the legality of norms.

10._____: a special type of formal organization characterized by centralized, hierarchically organized authority. It emphasizes impersonal work relationships, technical knowledge, and rationality.

11._____: the theory that recognizes formal and informal organization, and their relationship to each other. It also looks at the effects of the environment upon the organization and at economic and social rewards within the organization.

12._____: spontaneous groups that emerge usually within formal organizations. They are often based upon unofficial and often implicit rules or understandings.

13._____: Weber's idea that there existed an historical tendency to bring more and more aspects of social life under the rule of rational, efficient, scientific thought.

14._____: according to Weber, authority which rests upon the belief that a leader has special qualities and therefore should be obeyed.

15._____: in Weber's view, the process of rendering power acceptable to those affected by its exercise.

16._____: a social group in which relationships are instrumental, impersonal, rational, and efficient.

17._____: as applied to organizations the theory that examines their taken-for-granted, informal, often unconscious rules.

18._____: a relatively stable, patterned set of reciprocal relationships and expectations (social roles and norms) that creates the possibility of predictable behaviour.

19._____: social groups with a high division of labour, deliberately and consciously created to achieve specified goals.

20._____: Durkheim's conception of a social integration based on functional interdependence of social roles, characteristic of societies marked by a highly differentiated, complex division of labour.

21._____: according to Weber, authority based upon the conventions of past generations.

22._____: according to Marx, a distortion built into the structure of capitalism, in which workers are put into conflict with others and lose control of creative capacity, the productive process, and the product of their labour.

23._____: a small, voluntary work group that meets periodically to discuss work-related problems and recommend solutions.

24._____: Durkheim's conception of a social integration based on a homogeneity of values and behaviour, characteristic of societies marked by a simple division of labour.

25._____: a social group in which relationships are characterized by emotion, warmth, cooperation, and usually face-to-face interaction.

SELF QUIZ

1. Which is (are) not a dysfunction(s) of bureaucracies according to Merton?

   a) inflexibility
   b) displacement of goals
   c) the principle of office hierarchy
   d) mechanical solidarity
   e) c and d

2. According to Durkheim, a society which is based on a high degree of moral consensus, shared values, and sentiments is characterized by

   a) organic solidarity
   b) bureaucratic control
   c) harsh, punitive responses to deviance
   d) a complex division of labour
   e) a weak collective conscience

3. According to Durkheim, the major driving forces underlying all forms of social organization in contemporary society are

   a) division of labour and increased rationality
   b) class consciousness and power elites
   c) population density and industrialization
   d) bureaucracy and a weak collective conscience
   e) b and c

4. Lenin and Trotsky's explanation for the failure of the bureaucratic state to wither away following the Russian Revolution was

   a) the persistence of false consciousness among the workers
   b) the iron law of oligarchy
   c) that workers are motivated more by social rewards than by economic rewards
   d) that Russia was in a transitional stage between capitalism and communism
   e) that communism cannot succeed

5. People like John Kennedy and Pierre Trudeau are said to possess _____ authority.

   a) traditional
   b) charismatic
   c) ethnomethodological
   d) patriarchal
   e) leadership

6.   For Edwards, the third form of control of the labour process is called

a)   simple
b)   technical
c)   bureaucratic
d)   mechanical
e)   organic

7.   Which of the following is not a characteristic of Weber's concept of bureaucracy?

a)   expert training
b)   hierarchy
c)   flexible rules
d)   written documents
e)   official jurisdictional areas

8.   The main reason(s) for the tendency toward oligarchy according to Michels is (are)

a)   the psychological needs of the leaders to maintain power
b)   the need of workers to be motivated more by social than economic rewards
c)   the need of the public to be guided
d)   a and b
e)   a and c

9.   Which theoretical perspective could be accused of manipulating workers?

a)   ethnomethodology
b)   scientific management
c)   the human relations school
d)   bureaucratic theory
e)   new industrial sociology

10.   What general conclusion(s) can be drawn from the Hawthorne studies?

a)   the underlying model of human nature is that of a machine-like, rational being motivated by simple, economic needs
b)   production decreases when illumination of the workspace is decreased
c)   production decreases when rest periods are eliminated
d)   simply putting people in an experimental situation changes their behaviour
e)   b and c only

11.   Rinehart felt that sociologists should look not to _____ that claim(s) to measure worker alienation but to strikes, restriction of output, industrial sabotage, and humorous horseplay on the job.

a)   attitude questionnaires
b)   dysfunctions
c)   the informal organization
d)   the formal organization
e)   negotiated order theory

12.   Which is not a general source of resistance to quality circles?

a)   the fear of further Japanese encroachment into North American markets
b)   middle level managers who feel threatened
c)   the cultural gap between Japan and North America

d) organized labour
e) a and d

13. The theoretical foundation of negotiated order is found in

a) ethnomethodology
b) functionalism
c) symbolic interactionism
d) conflict theory
e) the writings of Cooley

14. If you were a person who liked fixed rules, set routines, and predictability, you would probably most dislike

a) the structural approach
b) the scientific management school
c) bureaucracies
d) negotiated order theory
e) ideal types

15. Mechanical solidarity can be found in societies

a) that are characterized by a complex division of labour
b) in which role conflicts are abundant
c) in which individuals share similar values and beliefs
d) that are scientifically and technically oriented
e) none of the above

FILL IN THE BLANKS

1. The idea of a social construction of reality is most relevant to the _____ aspect of organization.

2. A special type of formal organization, one particularly characteristic of the modern world, and sometimes called "the iron cage" is a _____.

3. For individuals, contact with formal organizations is often frustrating, impersonal, and _____.

4. The invention of a money economy, the growth and centralization of capital, and the creation of increasingly larger businesses and unions went hand in hand with the development of _____.

5. Bureaucracies are held together by _____ solidarity.

6. Families and friendship groups are examples of _____ groups.

7. A bureaucracy is an excellent example of Cooley's _____ group.

8.   _____ was Weber's concept for the movement away from magical or sacred interpretations of the world.

9.   Weber saw _____ authority as the type underlying modern bureaucracy.

10. Individuals who violate group norms by over-producing are called

_____.

11. The earliest form of control according to Edwards was called _____ control and often involved a single entrepreneur.

12. In his book, *Wealth of Nations,* _____ used the manufacture of pins as an example of how production can be increased through specialization.

13. Social philosophers before Durkheim saw society as held together by a

_____.

14. According to the human relations school, _____ incentives are not the most important determinants of production rates. _____ factors have a greater influence upon how much is produced.

15. Negotiated order theory argues that the formal rules found in organizations are neither very extensive nor explicit and that organizational personnel frequently do not know all the rules or how and when to apply them. Consequently, the rules are treated as general _____, the specific meaning of which must be worked out in concrete situations.

ANSWERS

KEY TERMS AND DEFINITIONS

1.	new industrial sociology	10.	bureaucracy
2.	ideal type	11.	structuralism
3.	iron law of oligarchy	12.	informal organizations
4.	scientific management	13.	rationalization
5.	division of labour	14.	charismatic authority
6.	negotiated order theory	15.	legitimation
7.	social contract	16.	secondary group
8.	human relations school	17.	ethnomethodology
9.	rational-legal authority	18.	organization

19. formal organizations
20. organic solidarity
21. traditional authority
22. alienation

23. quality circle
24. mechanical solidarity
25. primary group

SELF QUIZ

1. e
2. c
3. a
4. d
5. b

6. c
7. c
8. e
9. c
10. d

11. a
12. a
13. c
14. d
15. c

FILL IN THE BLANKS

1. subjective
2. bureaucracy
3. alienating
4. formal organization
5. organic
6. primary
7. secondary
8. Disenchantment of the world
9. rational-legal
10. rate busters
11. simple
12. Adam Smith
13. social contract
14. economic, Social
15. understandings or guidelines

CHAPTER 14

Social Movements

OBJECTIVES

1. To understand what is meant by the general term collective behaviour and its specific forms: panics, crowds, fads, crazes, publics, and social movements.

2. To understand the collective behaviour perspective on social movements including Blumer's and Smelser's work as well as emergent-norm theory and game theory.

3. To compare and contrast other theoretical perspectives on social movements — the social breakdown approach, the relative deprivation approach, and the collective action approach.

4. To be aware of the principal cleavages and integrative bonds that have shaped the character of collective action in Canada, with emphasis on regional and ethnic cleavages.

KEY TERMS AND DEFINITIONS

1. _____: activity in which a large number of people reject and/or do not conform to conventional ways of acting. Behaviour of this kind is often described as less "institutionalized" than ordinary behaviour.

2. _____: a large and dispersed group made up of persons who share an interest in the same thing. They may hold similar views, or they may sharply disagree.

3. _____: large collectivities of people trying to bring about or resist social change. Sociologists often assume that they are the most institutionalized form of collective behaviour.

4. _____: a special type of interaction in which responses are reinforced among people. The behaviour of one individual stimulates a response in another person, which in turn reinforces the tendency of the first person, and so on.

5. _____: over-simplified notions that, according to Smelser, give rise to collective behaviour. They portray the world in terms of omnipotent forces, conspiracies, or extravagant promises.

6. _____: the attachment of individuals to social groups or institutions. It depends on a set of sanctions that rewards conformity to groups' norms and punishes non-conformity.

7. _____: an explanation of crowd behaviour which stresses diversity of membership, but a perception of consensus that leads to a new norm expressing the apparent will of the crowd.

8. _____: an approach to collective behaviour that argues that social unrest occurs when established institutions are disrupted or weakened.

9. _____: the rapid and uncontrolled spread of a mood, impulse, or form of conduct through a collectivity of people.

10. _____: an explanation of crowd behaviour similar to emergent-norm theory, except that it assumes that people conduct themselves in a "rational" manner and on the basis of relative costs and payoffs.

11. _____: a movement in the 1960s in Quebec to expand governmental powers, to decrease church power, to modernize Quebec, and to fight vigorously for *la survivance*.

12. _____: the pursuit of goals by more than one person. As an explanation of social movements, it looks at integration and cleavage factors and seeks to explain what is dissimilar about collective action at different times and in different places.

13. _____: the transfer of resources, particularly human resources, from the pursuit of one goal or set of goals to the pursuit of another goal or set of goals.

14. _____: an unconventional practice that is adopted by a large number of individuals, but is regarded as strange by most people in the society. It is generally more outlandish than a fad, and therefore requires greater personal commitment.

15. _____: a division (based on age, class, or ethnicity, etc.) that may result in the formation of distinct social groups.

16. _____: a temporary group of people in reasonably close physical proximity. Only unconventional ones are included under the heading of collective behaviour.

17. _____: a relatively well-articulated statement of beliefs and objectives that can be used to justify patterns of conduct. It often identifies "wrongs" in a society and offers a remedy for correcting them.

18. _____: an unconventional practice that spreads rapidly and is adopted in a short period of time by a large number of people. It is generally less outlandish than a craze, and therefore requires less personal commitment.

19. _____: the difference between what people believe they have a right to receive (their *expectations*) and what they actually receive (their *achievements*).

20._____: a rapid and impulsive course of action that occurs when people are frightened and try to save themselves or their property from perceived danger.

21._____: survival of French Canada as a distinct society.

22._____: the individual benefits that a person can derive from belonging to an association or joining a social movement. They help motivate people to join social movements.

23._____: a set of beliefs which helps people to interpret and explain their world and which provides the basis for collective action

24._____: the domination of a class or classes over others, not only economically but politically and culturally as well

25._____: a pattern of relationships among individuals or groups in a society that usually changes only slowly. For example, the kinship structure of a society refers to the most commonly found relations among relatives and married persons in a society. Social stratification is the structure of inequality in a society.

SELF QUIZ

1.   The general term given to the human activity that may occur when a large number of people does not accept some of the prevailing values, norms, and/or leaders in a society is

    a)   a public
    b)   a craze
    c)   a panic
    d)   collective behaviour
    e)   a crowd

2.   _____ is usually the major reason that people engage in protest activities.

    a)   Social cleavage
    b)   Anger
    c)   Relative deprivation
    d)   Rising expectations
    e)   Social integration

3.   Blumer argued that the fundamental process(es) underlying crowd behaviour is (are)

    a)   interpretive behaviour
    b)   panic
    c)   social contagion
    d)   circular reaction
    e)   c and d only

4.   Which of the following does not describe new social movements?

   a) social breakdown
   b) anti-authority
   c) less economic than old movements
   d) concerned with values and culture
   e) spontaneous and decentralized

5.   Which of the following is (are) a criticism of Smelser's work?

   a) there is insufficient evidence to show that circular reaction is characteristic of collective behaviour
   b) the suggestion that participants are swept up in a common mood is not demonstrated
   c) it implies that the motivations and aims of those who engage in collective behaviour are the illusions of irrational minds
   d) a and b only
   e) a and c only

6.   Bourassa thought the special mission of French Canadians was to preserve above all their

   a) language
   b) culture
   c) religion
   d) institutions
   e) economy

7.   Which of the following is a criticism of the collective behaviour tradition?

   a) too much attention is given to social structure
   b) too little attention is spent on interest groups and on the conflict among such groups
   c) too much attention is spent on mobilization factors
   d) it ignores the distinguishing feature of social movements, that is, their lack of institutionalization
   e) none of the above

8.   According to the collective-action perspective, two kinds of factors are necessary for the occurrence of social movements. They are

   a) social breakdown and relative deprivation
   b) discontent and consensus
   c) cleavage factors and integrating factors
   d) mobilization factors and discontent
   e) social breakdown factors and socially isolated individuals

9.   De Tocqueville thought that a major factor underlying the French Revolution was

   a) rising expectations
   b) discontent
   c) dissatisfaction
   d) circular reaction
   e) contagion

10. Social cleavage between regions, combined with social integration within regions has resulted in collective action that tends to be weak and divided _____, while often strong _____.
    a) nationally, regionally
    b) regionally, nationally
    c) individually, socially
    d) politically, economically
    e) b and d

11. Nationally, the Progressive Movement did not survive long as an independent political force because
    a) it relied too heavily on religious broadcasts to attract followers
    b) its leader died and the routinization of charisma failed
    c) it was too local, drawing its strength primarily from the Prairie provinces
    d) it was taken over by the CCF
    e) b and c

12. Which political party charged that eastern business elites were controlling and manipulating the economy to serve their interests?
    a) CCF
    b) NDP
    c) Social Credit
    d) Communist
    e) none of the above

13. Who focus on differences and discontinuities; they denounce positivism and stress indeterminacy; and they reject large embracing theories that try to explain everything?
    a) postmodernists
    b) neo-Marxists
    c) collective action theorists
    d) relative deprivation theorists
    e) game theorists

14. The point of the boxed insert on food rioters is that crowd behaviour is
    a) wild and senseless
    b) logically patterned
    c) evolutionary
    d) more like a craze than a fad
    e) contracultural

15. Nationalism as an ideology has long been popular among the people of Quebec. The survival of French Canada, before the Quiet Revolution, was to be achieved by
    a) advocating separation from the rest of Canada
    b) keeping people loyal to traditional values
    c) strengthening ties with France
    d) accepting the processes of urbanization and industrialization
    e) maintaining tight control over the provincial government

FILL IN THE BLANKS

1.   In contrast to relative deprivation theory, collective action argues that discontent is perhaps a _____ condition but not a _____ condition for social unrest.

2.   In resource mobilization theory, the function of a _____ is to identify a problem, diagnose it, attribute blame and offer a solution.

3.   According to social breakdown theory, _____, _____ and _____, individuals are most likely to participate in social unrest.

4.   Collective action theorists argue that it is more important to study the _____ rather than the amount of social unrest.

5.   The two categories of revolts in which Marxists are interested are those that led to the overthrow of _____ and those that Marx hoped would lead to the overthrow of _____.

6.   The theory that can best explain why many different types of people would all begin to believe in something like the necessity for eating certain foods is _____.

7.   Ideology, leadership, effective means of communication, cooperative relationships, and financial resources are each part of the larger process of _____, a key factor of the collective action approach.

8.   There is a widespread supposition in sociological writings that social unrest occurs when established institutions are _____.

9.   One of the significant contributions of Gramsci has been to persuade Marxists of the importance of _____ struggles against the existing order.

10.   Until the 1990s considerable _____ characterized collective action by Indians and Inuit in Canada which allowed other Canadians to rule them without serious opposition.

11.   _____ refers to relatively non-institutionalized conduct, i.e., conduct that departs from the ordinary and routine. In contrast, _____ covers both institutionalized and non-institutionalized activity.

12.   The major _____ are the student, urban, feminist, environmental, gay and lesbian ones.

13.   We learn about the views of a _____ by studying the results of political elections, calls to phone-in shows, letters to newspapers, etc.

14. The "Regina Manifesto" is associated with the _____.

15. Those patterns of differentiation that have had the most effect on collective action in Canada are: _____, _____, _____, _____, _____, and _____.

_____

ANSWERS

KEY TERMS AND DEFINITIONS

1. collective behaviour
2. public
3. social movements
4. circular reaction
5. generalized beliefs
6. social integration
7. emergent-norm theory
8. social breakdown approach
9. social contagion
10. game theory
11. Quiet Revolution
12. collective action
13. mobilization
14. craze
15. social cleavage
16. crowd
17. ideology
18. fad
19. relative deprivation
20. panic
21. *la survivance*
22. selective incentives
23. frame
24. hegemony
25. social structure

SELF QUIZ

1. d
2. b
3. e
4. a
5. c
6. c
7. b
8. c
9. a
10. a
11. c
12. c
13. a
14. b
15. b

FILL IN THE BLANKS

1. necessary, sufficient
2. frame
3. alienated, uprooted, socially maladjusted
4. character

5. feudalism, capitalism
6. emergent-norm theory
7. mobilization
8. disrupted or weakened
9. non-economic including ideological
10. factionalism
11. Collective behaviour, collective action
12. new social movements
13. public
14. CCF
15. age, socioeconomic status or class, ethnicity, region, rural or urban residence, gender

CHAPTER 15

Demography and Population Study

OBJECTIVES

1.   To understand the basic variables of population study — fertility, mortality, and migration — and the part each plays in the development of society.

2.   To understand two theoretical perspectives on population change — demographic transition theory and the views of Thomas Malthus.

3.   To appreciate the historical background of the growth of Canada's population.

4.   To learn how to measure mortality, fertility, and migration, and to be aware of factors related to these variables in the Canadian context.

KEY TERMS AND DEFINITIONS

1. _____: also called degenerative diseases, these illnesses are usually found in middle and old age, and relate to the body wearing out. These are the principal causes of death in industrial societies.

2. _____: also called infectious diseases, these illnesses are communicable from person to person and were the major causes of death prior to the twentieth century.

3. _____: the average number of years individuals of a given age can expect to live in the future.

4. _____: checks to population growth, such as vice, war, famine, and disease; posited by Malthus. They raise the death rate.

5. _____: the number of males in a given population per 100 females in that population. At birth around the world it is 105.

6. _____: the number of births to women of a particular age group divided by the total number of women of that age.

7. _____: the number of births per year per 1000 people.

8. _____: the movement of people across a significant boundary for the purpose of permanent settlement.

9. _____: checks to population growth that prevent the birth of children, such as abstinence and late marriage; posited by Malthus.

10._____: a model of population change that describes the movement of a society from relatively high fertility and mortality levels to relatively low ones.

11._____: the increase in population that occurs when fertility exceeds mortality. This condition has prevailed throughout most of human history.

12._____: the number of deaths of people of a particular age group divided by the total number of people of that age; usually arranged in five-year intervals.

13._____: from the Greek *demos* meaning people, it is the science of human numbers in terms of size, distribution, composition, and change.

14._____: the number of deaths per year per 1000 people.

15._____: a graphic representation of the age (usually in five-year intervals) and sex composition of a population.

16._____: the age-specific death rate for infants who die in the first year of life.

SELF QUIZ

1.   The world is adding one billion people about every _____ years.
  a) 100
  b) 50
  c) 36
  d) 12
  e) 2

2.   Stage I of the demographic transition is characterized by
  a) high fertility, low mortality
  b) low fertility, low mortality
  c) high fertility, high mortality
  d) low fertility, high mortality
  e) none of the above

3.   Today's developing nations are at a disadvantage in trying to duplicate the European experience of the demographic transition because
  a) the dramatic decrease in mortality occurred too quickly for them
  b) there is a dramatic increase in their fertility but not a corresponding increase in mortality
  c) new methods of birth control are required there
  d) they are stuck in stage I of the demographic transition
  e) they prefer positive to preventive checks

4. Malthus based his ideas on the relationship of population to the social and economic world. Which of the following is not one of his arguments?

    a) population invariably increases when the means of subsistence increase
    b) new methods of birth control for males must be developed to keep population in check
    c) population is necessarily limited by the means of subsistence
    d) checks to population growth include vice, war, and famine
    e) some increase in population is necessary because having children keeps people working for progress

5. _____ has (have) always been the major determinant of population growth in Canada.

    a) Emigration
    b) Immigration
    c) Mortality
    d) Positive checks
    e) Natural increase

6. Which of the following is a criticism of Malthusian theory?

    a) he overestimated the advances the Industrial and Agricultural Revolutions would make possible
    b) he defined the level of subsistence too specifically
    c) he could not foresee the possibility of birth control technology and its widespread application
    d) he focused his attention too heavily on the capitalist structure rather than on individual initiative
    e) b and d

7. Of the following, which variable has been the most important factor in the growth of the Canadian population?

    a) migration
    b) immigration
    c) emigration
    d) fertility
    e) b and c

8. According to age-specific death rates, mortality is relatively high

    a) during the first year of life
    b) for ages 10-14
    c) for ages 40-54
    d) in all years of life
    e) for women in childbearing years

9. Deaths in the first month of life are

    a) three-quarters of the total of infant deaths
    b) hard to prevent
    c) probably due to biological factors
    d) probably due to cultural factors
    e) a, b, and c

10. According to mortality differentials, which of the following individuals of equal age is probably likely to die first?

    a) a married male from a middle socioeconomic status
    b) a divorced female of French origin
    c) a single male from a low socioeconomic status
    d) a married female from a low socioeconomic status
    e) a divorced male from a middle socioeconomic status

11. Which of the following is overall the most important explanatory factor in variations of number of children born?

    a) ethnic background
    b) social class
    c) rural/urban location
    d) education
    e) age of marriage/marriage duration

12. Which of the following is true?

    a) foreign-born women in Canada today have many more children than those women who are born in Canada
    b) there is a consistent inverse relationship between education and fertility
    c) the differences in fertility between rural and urban residents is greater today than in the past
    d) the differences in fertility among religious groups is more important for younger women (under 30) than for older women
    e) there is no direct relationship between income and fertility except at older ages where higher levels of income are associated with having more children

13. Canada's crude birth rate today is about

    a) 38
    b) 28
    c) 23
    d) 13
    e) 3

14. Which of the following is true?

    a) older adults are more likely to make multiple migrations than young adults
    b) men tend to migrate more often than women
    c) the less education one has, usually the more mobile one is
    d) professionals are more likely to migrate than unskilled labourers
    e) the terms migrant and mover are essentially interchangeable

15. A population-pyramid

    a) provides information on the average number of years any individual can expect to live upon reaching a certain age
    b) reveals if a society has an old or a young population
    c) allows one to study society in terms of size, distribution, composition, and change
    d) gives information pertaining to the movement of people across a significant boundary
    e) gives information pertaining to the number of births and deaths per year in a population

FILL IN THE BLANKS

1. Demography's primary variables are _____, _____, and _____.

2. Malthus argued that if unchecked, population grows _____, while food grows arithmetically.

3. It is clear that population growth on a world scale is a function of the relationship between _____ and _____.

4. The demographic transition can be summarized as follows:

    Stage I: _____ fertility + _____ mortality = _____ increase.

    Stage II: _____ fertility + _____ mortality = _____ increase.

    Stage III: _____ fertility + _____ mortality = _____ increase.

5. "The Broken Heart" made the point that _____ was one route to reducing chances of premature death.

6. Malthus was not only a demographer but a _____.

7. Currently, the Canadian population is growing at slightly more than one percent per year. About two thirds of that increase is accounted for by _____, one third by _____.

8. It should be noted that most of Canada's population growth is due to the _____ of immigrants and their descendants, and not to _____ per se.

9. Overall, about 70 percent of Canada's population lives on about _____ percent of its land.

10. For younger people, the _____ is a preferred method of contraception while for older people it is _____.

11.   Some view the _____ rate as the single most important index of the level of modernization in society, in that low rates are indicative of sophisticated medical and nutritional systems.

12.   Two infectious diseases, today almost nonexistent, that formerly were the largest factors in mortality are _____ and _____.

13.   For women under 30, the major variables associated with low fertility differences are high _____ levels and _____ participation. Among older women, the social factors most important in explaining fertility variations are rural/urban residence, _____, and _____.

14.   A composite picture of the very mobile person in Canadian society would be one of either sex, recently _____, between the ages of _____, with some _____ training, and working as a _____.

15.   The change from a young to an old national population is accounted for primarily through _____ fertility and then a stabilization of the birth rate at a _____ level.

16.   The basic causes of migration have been classified as _____ factors. Undesirability of the place of origin is an example of the former while the desire to follow friends is an example of the latter.

ANSWERS

KEY TERMS AND DEFINITIONS

1. chronic diseases
2. acute diseases
3. life expectancy
4. positive checks
5. sex ratio
6. age-specific birth rate
7. crude birth rate
8. migration

9. preventive checks
10. demographic transition
11. natural increase
12. age-specific death rate
13. demography
14. crude death rate
15. population pyramid
16. infant mortality rate

SELF QUIZ

1. d
2. c
3. a
4. b
5. e

6. c
7. d
8. a
9. e
10. c

11. e
12. b
13. d
14. d
15. b

FILL IN THE BLANKS

1. fertility, mortality, migration
2. geometrically or by doubling
3. fertility, mortality
4   high, high, low; high, low, rapid; low, low, low
5. love and companionship
6. minister
7. natural increase, migration
8. fertility, immigration
9. one
10. pill, sterilization
11. infant mortality
12. TB, pneumonia
13. educational, labour force, religion, ethnicity
14. married, 25-29, university, professional
15. declining, low
16. push and pull

CHAPTER 16

Urban Sociology

OBJECTIVES

1. To understand the origin of cities and the patterns of Canadian urban settlement.

2. To learn something about the differences between rural and urban communities and the effects of suburbanization on the urban landscape.

3. To be familiar with human ecological explanations of the organization of the city, including three specific perspectives — concentric zone theory, sector theory, and multiple nuclei theory.

4. To understand two additional theoretical perspectives in urban sociology: the social choice (value orientation) school, and the social power school.

5. To be aware of the problems involved with urban renewal, urban housing, and crime.

KEY TERMS AND DEFINITIONS

1. _____: a theoretical perspective developed to explain changes in the social structure of the city based on the principle of competition for scarce resources and land. This competition results in a number of processes including centralization, concentration, segregation, invasion, and succession.

2. _____: the growth of cities, due to reclassification of rural areas, natural population increase, and/or movement from rural areas to cities.

3. _____: the theory of urban growth proposing that a central core, a zone in transition, and increasingly affluent neighborhoods radiate from the centre of the city outward.

4. _____: the theory of urban development that sees city land-use patterns characterized by wedge-like sectors that begin at the centre of the city and follow transportation routes outward.

5. _____: a theory of urban development that sees a number of centres developing in the city around specialized facilities.

6. _____: building and neighborhood construction designed to discourage crime by increasing interaction between residents and consequently public surveillance.

7. _____: communities that emerge from the competition for space in cities, characterized by their populations having homogeneous social characteristics.

8. _____: an explanation of crime which argues that the convergence in space and time of motivated offenders, suitable targets (victims), and the absence of capable guardians increases the probability of crime victimization.

SELF QUIZ

1. Which was not included among the four main types of settlements that historically appeared in Canada?

    a) colonial *entrepôt*
    b) border city
    c) commercial centre
    d) commercial industrial city
    e) metropolitan community

2. Gentrification and white-painting are aspects of

    a) the return of the middle class to inner cities
    b) the rural renaissance
    c) sector theory
    d) the ecological fallacy
    e) urban emigration patterns

3. According to Davis which of the following is the main source of urban growth?

    a) the city's greater natural increase
    b) declines in mortality
    c) values increasing fertility
    d) movement from the country to the city
    e) positive checks

4. Park and Burgess, two of the leading figures in the development of the human ecology perspective on urban change, argued that there are dynamic processes at work in the city which allow new communities to emerge. One of these processes is

    a) stratification
    b) organization
    c) nationalization
    d) competition
    e) the ecological fallacy

5. Which of the following is not one of the processes enumerated by human ecology theory?

    a) invasion
    b) centralization
    c) decentralization
    d) succession
    e) defensible space

6. The ecological fallacy refers to making inferences about

   a) characteristics of an area or group based on the characteristics of individuals
   b) changes in the social structure of a city based on the principles of competition for scarce resources
   c) characteristics of individuals based on the characteristics of an area or group
   d) land resources based on the characteristics of past surplus and shortages
   e) none of the above

7. Five major differences between rural and urban communities have been identified by Poplin. Which of the following is not part of his distinction?

   a) urbanites enjoy more anonymity than ruralites
   b) rural areas are characterized by a greater division of labour
   c) urban communities tend to be more heterogeneous
   d) impersonal relationships are likely to flourish in the urban setting
   e) in rural communities, people tend to evaluate others on the basis of their personal characteristics

8. In human ecology terms, movement to the suburbs is an aspect of

   a) concentration
   b) deconcentration
   c) invasion
   d) decentralization
   e) none of the above

9. Which perspective focussed on the neighborhood as an area in which special interests develop and on the distribution and allocation of municipal resources?

   a) social choice
   b) social area analysis
   c) human ecology, specifically concentric zone theory
   d) social power school
   e) technological school

10. Unlike the feudal order, industrial urban society has all of the following except

    a) inanimate sources of energy
    b) an emphasis on achievement
    c) scientific applications
    d) less diffused social power
    e) b and d

11. Broken windows, abandoned buildings, and loitering teenagers were described as marks of

    a) defensible space
    b) individuality and eccentricity
    c) incivility
    d) urban renewal
    e) segregation

12. According to Murdie's study of Toronto, all three human ecology theories were applicable. Ethnic clustering was used as evidence to support which one?
    a) concentric zone
    b) sector
    c) multiple nuclei
    d) social power
    e) none of the above

FILL IN THE BLANKS

1. North American and European cities share a problem with those of Africa and Asia, but in the opposite direction. This is the problem of a _____.

2. São Paolo directly contradicts the _____ theory of urban development.

3. Projecting to 2001, demographers predict that _____ to _____ percent of Canada's population will be urban.

4. Burgess argued that cities grow outward in circles from the CBD. Those initials stand for the _____.

5. The tendency for selected institutions and services to cluster near the city's focal points of transportation is called _____ in human ecology theory.

6. The tendency for various groups and institutions to locate in separate and distinct parts of the city is called _____ in human ecology theory.

7. According to concentric zone theory, immigrant groups tend to settle first in the zone of _____ and then as they prosper, move outwards, some eventually landing in the _____ zone.

8. To assume that all people living in high crime areas are criminals is to commit the _____.

9. Wirth argued that the continued growth of American cities, their increasing density, and their increasing mixture of ethnic, occupational, and income groups all would combine to create social environments in which there would be _____, _____, and social _____. Gans disagreed.

10. In cities, people frequently judge others' status based on the _____, the type of cars they drive, and the _____. In rural communities, on the other hand, people tend to know each other personally.

11. On the overall quality of life index the city of _____ has the highest score while _____ has the lowest.

12.   One of the biggest problems of urban renewal for residents is _____.

ANSWERS

KEY TERMS AND DEFINITIONS

1. human ecology
2. urbanization
3. concentric zone theory
4. sector theory

5. multiple nuclei theory
6. defensible space
7. natural areas
8. routine activities theory

SELF QUIZ

1. b
2. a
3. d
4. d

5. e
6. c
7. b
8. b

9. d
10. d
11. c
12. c

FILL IN THE BLANKS

1. highly dependent population (young in Asia, old in North America and Europe)
2. rural renaissance
3. 80, 85
4. central business district
5. centralization
6. segregation
7. transition, commuter
8. ecological fallacy
9. loneliness, alienation, deviance
10. neighborhoods in which they live, clothes they wear
11. Calgary, Montreal
12. a loss of contact and support from friends